SERIAL KILLERS

Joseph James DeAngelo

The Golden State Killer

by Rebecca Morris

Essential Library

An Imprint of Abdo Publishing

abdobooks.com

ABDOBOOKS.COM

Published by Abdo Publishing, a division of ABDO, PO Box 398166, Minneapolis, Minnesota 55439.

Printed in China.
102024
012025

THIS BOOK CONTAINS RECYCLED MATERIALS

Cover Photo: Sacramento County Sheriff's Department/Getty Images News/Getty Images
Interior Photos: Scott McPartland/Archive Photos/Getty Images, 4–5; Susan Law Cain/Shutterstock Images, 9; Shutterstock Images, 12–13; FBI, 16, 26, 32, 47, 51, 68–69; US Navy/Naval History and Heritage Command, 18; Jeff Pachoud/AFP/Getty Images, 20–21; Santiago Mejia/AFP/Getty Images, 24, 35; Santa Barbara County Sheriff's Office, 28; FBI/AP Images, 30–31, 52; Santiago Mejia/San Francisco Chronicle/AP Images, 39, 44–45; Visalia Police Department, 40; Mike Slaughter/Toronto Star/Getty Images, 55; Sundry Photography/Alamy, 56–57; Nick Otto/The Washington Post/Getty Images, 58; Paul Kitagaki Jr./Sacramento Bee/Tribune News Service/Getty Images, 63; Randy Pench/Sacramento Bee/Tribune News Service/Getty Images, 65, 90–91; Rachel Gunby/Shutterstock Images, 66; TEK Image/Science Source, 75; Jeff Chiu/AP Images, 76; Marmaduke St. John/Alamy, 78–79; Dimitrios Kambouris/Getty Images for TIME/Getty Images Entertainment/Getty Images, 82; Justin Sullivan/Getty Images News/Getty Images, 88; Paul Kitagaki Jr./The Sacramento Bee/AP Images, 92; Daniel Kim/Sacramento Bee/Tribune News Service/Getty Images, 95; Citizen of the Planet/Universal Images Group/Getty Images, 99

Editor: Marley Richmond
Series Designer: Joshua Olson

Library of Congress Control Number: 2024938309

PUBLISHER'S CATALOGING-IN-PUBLICATION DATA

Names: Morris, Rebecca, author.
Title: Joseph James DeAngelo: the Golden State killer / by Rebecca Morris
Other title: the Golden State killer
Description: Minneapolis, Minnesota: ABDO Publishing, 2025 | Series: Serial killers | Includes online resources and index.
Identifiers: ISBN 9781098295363 (lib. bdg.) | ISBN 9798384916369 (ebook)
Subjects: LCSH: DeAngelo, Joseph James, 1945- --Juvenile literature. | Golden State Killer--Juvenile literature. | Killers (Murderers)--Biographies--Juvenile literature. | Serial killers--Biographies--Juvenile literature. | Crime--Juvenile literature. | True crime stories--Juvenile literature.
Classification: DDC 364.15232--dc23

CONTENTS

This book discusses accounts of crime, violence, and death that may be disturbing to some readers.

CHAPTER 1

HOME ALONE

On the night of May 4, 1986, 18-year-old Janelle Cruz had just returned home from her shift at Bullwinkle's Restaurant, where she worked as a cashier. No one else was at the house. Cruz's mother, stepfather, and younger brother were on vacation in Cancún, Mexico, 3,000 miles (4,800 km) away.

Cruz and her family lived in Irvine, California, a city just south of Los Angeles. Their home was a single-story house on a cul-de-sac. Bushes surrounded the yard, and there was a pathway to a local park behind the house.

Janelle Cruz's family home was near several parks in Irvine, California. These parks may have provided an escape route for her attacker.

northwood community park
the city of irvine

Cruz had only recently moved back to Irvine for the summer. For the previous ten months, she had been in Utah working at ski slopes through the Job Corps. The Job Corps is a government program that assists teens and young adults with education and work training. Back in Irvine, Cruz had signed up for classes at a local community college in addition to working at Bullwinkle's Restaurant.

On that May night, Cruz invited a friend over to keep her company. They passed the time talking. Twice they were interrupted by noises from outside. The first noise sounded like a door or gate closing. Cruz went to the window but did not see anything out of the ordinary. She told her friend, "I think it's just the cats," and closed the window's shutters.[1]

When they heard a noise again, it sounded like it was coming from the garage. This time, Cruz said, "It's just the washing machine."[2] At 10:45 p.m., Cruz and her friend hugged goodbye, and the friend left.

A Horrific Discovery

The next afternoon, a real estate agent arrived at the home. Cruz's mother and stepfather were trying to sell the house, and the agent needed to make sure the home was ready to show to a potential buyer. When the agent arrived, she saw Cruz's beige Chevrolet Chevette in the driveway, but no one answered the doorbell. She got a key from the lockbox and opened the door.

The agent walked through the house. She passed two bedrooms before coming to a third room at the end of a hallway. It was Cruz's bedroom. Inside the bedroom, the agent could tell right away that something was wrong.

Cruz's body lay diagonal and unmoving on the bed. It was not the natural position of a person sleeping. A blanket covered the top half of Cruz's body. The bottom half of her body was unclothed. The scene shocked and frightened the agent. She feared an attacker might still be at the home.

She raced out of the house. Back at her office, the agent reported what she had seen to her boss. Two other agents went to the home to check on the situation. They confirmed a young woman had died at the home, and they called the police. The first to arrive was Barry Aninag, an officer with the Irvine Police Department. One of the real estate agents rushed from the kitchen to tell him, "There's a dead body in the bedroom. There's a dead body in the bedroom."[3]

> **"We never went back to that house. We sold it."[4]**
>
> ***—Michelle Cruz, Janelle Cruz's sister, in 2018***

At the scene, Officer Aninag found evidence of severe trauma to Cruz's head. The attacker had used a hard object to bludgeon her many times. There was a large wound on Cruz's forehead, and teeth were missing from her mouth. Her nose, eyes, and lips were bruised, and blood covered her face. Police also found evidence she had been raped.

Investigating the Scene

Police examined the house and interviewed Cruz's neighbors to gather information. Officers found blood on window shutters, on the floor near the front door, and on the kitchen floor and cabinets. They also found shoe prints outside the home.

Inside, police looked for a murder weapon. Cruz's family later told investigators that a pipe wrench had gone

A CONFESSION

A man named Greg Gonzalez had known Cruz years before her death. He said he had killed her. Gonzalez told a friend that he and Cruz had a fight, and then he hit her with a steel object. But at the end of the conversation, Gonzalez said the confession was a joke. The friend reported Gonzalez to the police. They arrested him on June 21, 1986. Police took blood and hair samples from Gonzalez and sent them to a laboratory for testing. The results did not match the samples from the crime scene. Police ruled Gonzalez out as a suspect.

When police interviewed Cruz's neighbors, two people reported an unusual amount of light coming from the Cruz house at 4:00 a.m. and at 5:30 a.m.

missing from their yard a few days before the murder. The metal tool had been by the back door. Investigators suspected the wrench was the murder weapon, but they never found it.

Police also never found ligatures, or materials used to bind Cruz, at the scene. However, there were shreds of cloth scattered over Cruz's body. Police suspected the attacker had positioned himself over Cruz and torn the material to create bindings, leaving shreds behind. Officer Larry Montgomery, the lead investigator on the case, suspected the killer had removed the bindings from the scene to avoid leaving them as evidence.

During the investigation, Cruz's family revealed more unsettling details to police. In the weeks before the attack, the family had received suspicious phone calls. The caller used a disguised voice and said, "I'm going to kill you."

MODUS OPERANDI

Law enforcement officers analyze crime scenes for patterns that give them insight into a criminal's behavior. These patterns are called *modus operandi*, which means "mode of operating" in Latin. Law enforcement uses the abbreviation MO for this term. Restraining a victim with a rope is an example of a criminal's MO. MOs can evolve as serial criminals commit more crimes. Recognizing an MO helps investigators link multiple cases to one suspect.

Cruz's mother, Diane Stein, described the voice as "low but almost childish."[5] The fake voice led the family to believe the calls were pranks.

Police looked into Cruz's acquaintances, her boyfriends, and the friend who had last seen her alive. However, officers did not uncover sufficient evidence to arrest anyone for her murder. Based on the crime scene, Officer Montgomery determined the police were searching for a very brutal type of killer. "This is a person who has a desire to hurt and to kill in a very violent hands-on way," he said.[6]

Decades of Mystery

Cruz's death remained unsolved for more than three decades. It was not until 2018, 32 years later, that investigators finally obtained the evidence they needed to identify the killer. His name was Joseph James DeAngelo.

By the time of his arrest, DeAngelo had committed 13 murders, approximately 50 rapes, and more than 120 burglaries. His crimes spanned many years, from the early 1970s to 1986, when Cruz became his final known victim. His crimes were spread throughout 11 counties from Northern to Southern California.[7]

Reporters and law enforcement agencies gave DeAngelo various nicknames throughout the years. These nicknames represented the different locations of his crimes and his escalation from trespasser to killer. They included the Visalia Ransacker, the East Area Rapist (EAR), and the Original Night Stalker (ONS). Paul Holes, a cold case investigator who worked for 24 years to identify the killer, described DeAngelo as one of history's worst serial killers.

PSYCHOLOGICAL PROFILE

Investigators use psychological profiles as tools to understand and identify serial criminals. Psychiatrists and psychologists, experts who specialize in behavior and mental illness, prepare these profiles. Dr. Kim Rossmo, a criminology professor, explains the three questions that guide these profiles: "What happened at the crime scene?" "Why did these actions occur?" "Who would have done this?" These questions help psychiatrists make predictions about the criminal. Predictions focus on factors such as the criminal's age, work history, lifestyle, and relationships. Nine psychological profiles were created while different law enforcement agencies worked to identify DeAngelo.

CHAPTER 2

AN UNSETTLED CHILDHOOD

Joseph James DeAngelo was born in Bath, New York, on November 8, 1945. He was named after his father, an officer in the US Air Force. His mother's name was Kathleen. Joseph had an older sister, Rebecca, and two younger siblings, Constance and John. The military career of Joseph DeAngelo Sr. meant the family moved often, both within the United States and abroad.

Difficult Family Life

Little is known about Joseph's life as a young child. The available information comes

Joseph James DeAngelo likely experienced childhood abuse. Childhood trauma, including abuse, is common in serial killers.

from family accounts and public records such as birth announcements. Property records show that Joseph grew up in a two-story apartment house in Bath.

According to family statements, Joseph saw and experienced abuse as a child. In one instance, he witnessed two airmen rape his seven-year-old sister, Constance. Joseph was about nine or ten years old, and the family was stationed at a military base in Germany. Joseph and Constance had been playing in a warehouse on the base when the attack occurred.

Decades later, Constance's son Jesse Ryland said that Kathleen and Joseph Sr. told the children not to talk about the rape. Ryland said his mother only revealed the attack to him while she was dying. She died in 2017, before her brother was identified as a serial rapist and killer.

RESEARCHING A KILLER

After DeAngelo's eventual arrest, journalist Neal Simon began to research DeAngelo's early life in Bath. Simon spoke to residents, but none had memories of DeAngelo as a boy. Simon also visited the site of the family's home. He discovered the local fire department had bought and then destroyed the home in a controlled burn in about 2006. Simon spoke with the local historical society and searched past newspapers for articles, announcements, or obituaries mentioning the DeAngelo family. The news sources had some details about noteworthy events in the lives of Kathleen and Joseph Sr. But much about the family's life remained unknown.

Ryland also said Constance told them abuse was common within the DeAngelo household. He said Joseph Sr. physically abused his wife and children. At times, he would lock his children in a closet as punishment and let them go hungry. Constance's other son, Wes Ryland, said that Joseph experienced more severe physical abuse than his siblings.

Jesse Ryland said that Kathleen was also physically abusive toward Constance. "She would hit my mom all the time," Jesse said. "I'm pretty positive [the children] were all abused like that."[1] It seems no one made official reports to police about claims of abuse in the family. Decades later, prosecutors did not find any recorded reports of abuse when looking into Joseph's early life.

Joseph Sr. was restationed to South Korea while Joseph Jr. was still in school. The rest of the family

JOSEPH JAMES DEANGELO SR.

Joseph James DeAngelo Sr. was stationed in the United States at least one more time after his assignment to South Korea. He eventually returned to South Korea, where he retired and later died. Little is known about the details of Joseph Sr.'s time in South Korea. One news source reports he died in 2000. Another reports he died in 1995. According to family members, Joseph Sr. had other children in South Korea. Family members said those children had the same names as three of his American children: Rebecca, Joseph, and Constance.

Rancho Cordova was not made into an official city of California until 2003. When DeAngelo's family moved there, Rancho Cordova was a small town.

remained in Rancho Cordova, California. Rancho Cordova is near Sacramento, toward the northern part of the state. Kathleen waitressed at the restaurant Denny's and started a relationship with another man, a welder named Percy John Bosanko Jr. Joseph's parents eventually divorced, and Kathleen married Bosanko.

Kathleen left many household responsibilities to Joseph during this time. Joseph's duties included watching his younger siblings and making sure they went to school, preparing meals, and doing laundry. During this time, Joseph and his mother had long arguments and shouted at one another.

High School Years

Joseph attended Mills Middle School and then Folsom High School. As a high school student, Joseph seemed to have two sides. On one, he had friends and hobbies. He played baseball on his high school's junior varsity team, did mechanical work on cars, and hunted rabbits with other boys in the rural areas around Rancho Cordova.

"Lots of serial killers develop gradually. A lot of them start with lesser offenses, develop to sex offenses and eventually murder."[3]

—James Alan Fox, professor of criminology, in 2018

Joseph's best friend in Rancho Cordova was from a large family of nine children. Joseph grew close to the friend's whole family. The boy's parents placed a class photograph of Joseph on a shelf alongside pictures of their own children. Joseph called the friend's parents "Mom" and "Pop."[2]

On the other side, Joseph was mysterious and shared little about himself. Despite being close with his friend's family, Joseph did not discuss his own life or feelings with them. Decades later, prosecutors reported Joseph

During his time serving in the Vietnam War, DeAngelo worked on board ships named the USS *Canberra, pictured*, and the USS *Piedmont*.

had a habit of trespassing, breaking into homes, and abusing animals as a teenager.

Military Service

In 1964, DeAngelo passed his General Educational Development (GED) tests, certifying that he had the equivalent knowledge to a person with a high school diploma. In September of that year, he enlisted in the US Navy. He completed his training at the Naval Training Center in San Diego, California. Then he served in the

Vietnam War (1954–1975) as a damage controlman. Damage controlmen in the US Navy do mechanical work on ships to maintain equipment and repair problems.

DeAngelo served two tours in the Vietnam War. A local newspaper ran an announcement along with a photograph of DeAngelo when he visited California on leave between the tours. DeAngelo received several medals for his time in the navy, including a National Defense Service Medal, a Vietnam Service Medal (Bronze Star), and a Vietnam Campaign Medal. DeAngelo was honorably discharged from the navy after four years. He returned to Northern California to live with his mother and stepfather.

A HAND INJURY IN VIETNAM

DeAngelo lost part of one ring finger during the years he was in the navy. He later told a girl he was dating that a bullet grazed his fingertip and caused the injury. However, an acquaintance said the injury happened in an accident with machinery on board a navy ship. The injury was visible throughout the rest of DeAngelo's life, but his victims did not report it in their physical descriptions of him. DeAngelo almost always wore gloves during his crimes.

CHAPTER 3

A BROKEN ENGAGEMENT

DeAngelo turned 23 years old in 1968, the same year he was discharged from the navy. Back in Northern California, he enrolled at Sierra College, a community college close to Rancho Cordova. DeAngelo took classes in police science, working toward his goal of becoming a law enforcement officer.

A College Romance

DeAngelo met Bonnie Jean Colwell at Sierra College. Colwell was 18 years old and planning to become a nurse. DeAngelo first approached Colwell when she was outside on the college's campus helping two young orphaned birds learn to fly. Caring for birds and other animals was part of her job as a lab assistant in the school's science department. After they met, DeAngelo started showing up at Colwell's job just to say hello to her. Soon the two began dating.

People studying police science often take forensics classes, where students may learn how to locate, preserve, and catalog evidence at crime scenes.

Colwell found DeAngelo to be outgoing and interesting. He met her friends and spent time with her family at their farm in Rancho Cordova. Colwell had four younger siblings, and DeAngelo took them to see movies at the drive-in theater. He tinkered with toy airplanes and built model boats for the children to enjoy. DeAngelo was adventurous. He took Colwell for rides on his motorcycle and brought her scuba diving.

DeAngelo also had another side that scared Colwell and made her feel uncomfortable. Sometimes when they went for rides on his motorcycle, DeAngelo would drive down dangerous paths at high speeds. On one of these

RANCHO CORDOVA

Rancho Cordova was an unincorporated community when DeAngelo grew up there. Unincorporated communities do not lie within the limits of a city. Rancho Cordova was a rural place surrounded by farmland and nature areas. DeAngelo knew the community well and knew how to avoid detection. For instance, he had played in Rancho Cordova's cement drainage canals as a teenager. These canals offered a quick path of escape. When committing his later crimes, DeAngelo often chose targets located close to these canals.

rides, Colwell saw DeAngelo kill a German shepherd by kicking the dog's neck. The dog had frequently chased and snapped at the passing motorcycle.

Colwell witnessed other disturbing behaviors as well. DeAngelo trespassed onto private property. He hunted illegally and handled the game in a way that made her feel uneasy, such as pulling a dove's meat off the bones with his hands after he shot it. Colwell also described long and painful sexual experiences with DeAngelo. She felt as though she had to do what DeAngelo wanted during their relationship, even when she was uncomfortable.

A Frightening Night

DeAngelo and Colwell became engaged in 1970. A local newspaper, the *Auburn Journal*, announced the engagement on May 14, 1970. That same year, DeAngelo graduated from Sierra College with an associate degree in police science. He then enrolled at California State

University, Sacramento, to pursue a bachelor's degree in criminal justice. Colwell transferred to the same university.

During the 1971 spring semester, DeAngelo and Colwell took the same abnormal psychology class. The class was a requirement for DeAngelo's criminal justice major, but he was failing it. He asked Colwell to help him cheat on an exam. Colwell said no, but DeAngelo continued to ask. He said she had to. Colwell called off their engagement and returned the ring DeAngelo had given her.

Two weeks went by, and then one night, a noise woke Colwell. It was a tapping sound against her window. She drew back the curtain and saw DeAngelo pointing a gun at her face. He said, "Get dressed."[1] He planned to take her to Reno, Nevada, so they could get married.

Colwell fled from her room and woke her father. He instructed her to hide in the bathroom while he confronted DeAngelo. "Don't you come out till I come to get you," he said to Colwell.[2] Colwell's father was a World War II (1939–1945) veteran who worked as a school principal. Colwell waited

"I was only 18 when we began dating and 19 when I ended it. . . . He was pushing me into fear and discomfort over and over again."[3]

—Bonnie Ueltzen (formerly Colwell), in 2020

When DeAngelo was eventually tried for his crimes, Bonnie Ueltzen (formerly Colwell) attended his trial.

in the bathroom for nearly two hours. Finally, her father came back and told her DeAngelo was gone. "You can go back to bed," her father said.[4]

After that night, Colwell left college for a semester because she was afraid of DeAngelo. When she returned, she switched her major to avoid seeing him. Colwell married someone else in 1972.

The Cordova Cat Burglar

DeAngelo continued studying for a police career after his engagement with Colwell ended. He graduated with a bachelor's degree in 1972 and then received additional training. He completed an advanced program called Peace Officer Standards and Training (POST) at the College of the Sequoias in Visalia, a small city more than 200 miles (320 km) south of Rancho Cordova. After completing that program, DeAngelo returned to the Rancho Cordova area and participated in an internship at the nearby Roseville Police Department.

While DeAngelo was training for a police career, a series of prowling activities and burglaries occurred in Rancho Cordova. Police started to receive break-in reports from these crimes in early 1972. As reports grew more frequent, police referred to the intruder as the Cordova Cat Burglar. A cat burglar is known for being agile and quiet with the ability to avoid detection. Such an intruder might climb through windows and onto roofs to enter homes. Although it would take decades, police eventually proved that the Cordova Cat Burglar was DeAngelo.

The Cordova Cat Burglar often sneaked in through side doors or sliding glass doors. Residents witnessed him jump from a house's roof and then leap over a fence to escape from the scene of a break-in. The cat burglar did not steal large items in these break-ins. He took coins from collections, small amounts of money, magnets, jewelry, or other small items.

Despite not resulting in expensive losses, the break-ins could be brutal. The cat burglar showed violence during these intrusions. At times, he would kill family dogs to stop them from barking, either by shooting them or by bludgeoning them. The *Grapevine*, Rancho Cordova's community newspaper, printed a story about these killings after a well-known neighborhood dog named Pups was attacked. Pups, who was ten years old, died from bludgeoning in February 1972.

There were also signs of a sexual component to the intrusions. Many of the break-ins occurred at night when residents were sleeping. The burglar crept into victims' bedrooms and watched them sleep. One woman woke to

Investigators believe that the Cordova Cat Burglar often escaped from crime scenes in thick bushes near the American River. The criminal may have climbed fences in order to hide.

find the burglar touching her chest. Sometimes the burglar stole photos of women and girls who lived in the homes, and he rifled through their underwear drawers.

The Cordova Cat Burglar committed dozens of break-ins, sometimes several in a single night. Police gathered evidence in hopes of catching him. One witness reported that the burglar drove a green Opel sedan. Another witness saw the burglar entering her home, so she got a weapon and confronted him. She gave police a physical description of the burglar for a composite sketch.

FRONT-PAGE NEWS

The *Exeter Sun*, a local newspaper, ran an article on its front page about DeAngelo when he joined the town's police department. The article's headline read, "Navy veteran serves Exeter as policeman."[6] The article featured a photograph of DeAngelo and provided biographical details about his life and military service. The article also reported DeAngelo's belief in "law and order" and his view of police work as "serving the community."[7]

The Cordova Cat Burglar break-ins continued in the first half of 1973. Throughout the police investigation, there was never reason to suspect DeAngelo as the perpetrator. He soon got his first police job. The Exeter Police Department hired him as an officer on May 18, 1973. Exeter was a rural town with a population of approximately 5,000 people located in Tulare County, the same county as Visalia.[5]

Officers who worked with DeAngelo on the Exeter police force remember him as being businesslike and overqualified for his position in such a small department.

The Beginning of a Double Life

The Exeter Police Department had ten officers when DeAngelo joined the force.[8] Because the department was small, officers often worked their shifts alone rather than with a partner. Nevertheless, the officers formed a close community. Farrel Ward, who worked alongside DeAngelo, described the department as being like a family. Ward noticed that DeAngelo was reserved and did not participate when the other officers told jokes and played games. DeAngelo "was always serious, always thinking, but was nice to people," Ward said.[9]

DeAngelo's duties as an officer in Exeter involved routine patrols for minor crimes and disturbances.

There were also times when he responded to serious crimes. An article in the *Exeter Sun* from July 11, 1973, mentioned DeAngelo as one of the officers who participated in the high-speed chase of a stolen car. Exeter officers, including DeAngelo, also assisted police departments in the nearby cities of Tulare County.

In the fall of 1973, a few months after joining the Exeter Police Department, DeAngelo married Sharon Marie Huddle. Huddle was a 20-year-old student at California State University, Fresno. She went on to become a lawyer during their marriage. Their wedding took place at the First Congregational Church in Auburn, California, close to where DeAngelo grew up. Huddle, similarly to DeAngelo's fellow officers, did not suspect DeAngelo of criminal activity. Their marriage was another sign of his double life.

TULARE COUNTY

Tulare County is in central California. Half the county is in the Central Valley, an agricultural area. The other half crosses into the Sierra Nevada. The county has eight cities, including Exeter, where DeAngelo had his first police job, and Visalia, where he completed his training at the College of the Sequoias. When DeAngelo worked in Exeter, Tulare's cities were small, and their police departments provided backup for one another. They also assisted the Tulare County Sheriff's Department.

CHAPTER 4

THE VISALIA RANSACKER

Exeter experienced an increase in home break-ins soon after DeAngelo joined the police department. On August 15, 1973, just three months after DeAngelo was hired, the *Exeter Sun* reported five burglaries in one week. Four occurred on a single day.[1] The details of these break-ins showed similarities with the Cordova burglaries. The intruder in Exeter stole small items such as coins and women's clothing. However, investigators did not connect the crimes in these two areas at the time.

Residents in nearby Visalia also experienced suspicious activity in the months after DeAngelo moved to Exeter. Prowling and ransacking reports grew frequent in the spring of 1974, with dozens of additional reports filed throughout the rest of that year and in 1975. Often there were reports of several incidents on the same day. Later, police, media, and residents referred to the perpetrator as

Photographs of the break-in crime scenes in Visalia show the thief rifled through victims' personal belongings, often leaving a mess behind.

the Visalia Ransacker. Similar to the Cordova Cat Burglar, detectives would eventually uncover that DeAngelo was behind this persona.

The Ransacker's Pattern

Crime scenes showed the ransacker had a unique and consistent pattern. The ransacker often entered homes when residents were not there. He went in

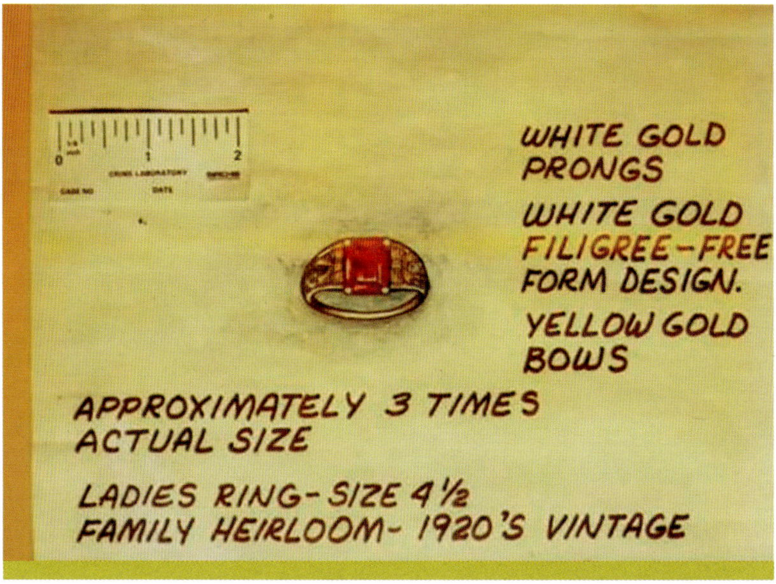

Investigators collected information about the items taken from victims' homes. One sketch showed details of a stolen ring.

through unlocked doors or pried open windows if they were locked.

Once inside, the ransacker took measures to avoid detection. He opened more windows to listen for anyone approaching the home. The open windows also gave the ransacker several exit options to escape the scene. He placed dishes or other breakable items against doors; these objects would alert the ransacker with a rattle or crash if someone tried to enter the home.

The ransacker stole small and unusual items from the homes he burglarized. He took perfume, jewelry, and coins or stamps from collections. When he stole jewelry, the pieces were often personalized or meaningful to the owner. For example, he took a locket with a photograph inside, a silver bracelet, and a wedding ring. In some break-ins, the ransacker stole items he could use for his crimes, including guns, ammunition, and tools such as a hammer.

The ransacker did extensive damage to the homes during his break-ins. He rummaged through bedroom dressers and closets, throwing clothing on the floor. He emptied medication into sinks, knocked over bookshelves, and stained carpets with wine and furniture with shaving cream. He went through kitchens and ate ice cream from people's freezers. One homeowner said, "Everything in that house was out. . . . Every kitchen drawer, everything, dumped on the floor."[2]

Similar to the Cordova Cat Burglar, the Visalia Ransacker rifled through women's underwear. He took undergarments from drawers and left them scattered around the house or arranged in patterns. Police investigating the crimes started to recognize one of the ransacker's signatures as a stack of undergarments on the bed alongside a screen taken from the window. Sometimes the ransacker

"The [Visalia Ransacker] tended to steal items important to his victims rather than gain financially from his crimes."[3]

—Visaliaransacker.com, an online database about the ransacker's crimes

took undergarments and photographs of women and girls from the homes when he left.

Gathering Evidence

Residents who saw the ransacker described him to police. Police compiled the common details to issue a description of the suspect. According to the description, he was a white man with blond hair. He was about five feet, ten inches (1.78 m) tall, weighed 180 to 200 pounds (82–91 kg), and was 25 to 35 years old. Witnesses also reported that the ransacker appeared to be strong. He had the ability to run from crime scenes and jump fences.

"Visalia was a very small town at the time. . . . People started turning in friends and relatives, and the department looked at hundreds of people for the crimes."[4]

—Terry Ommen, local historian and former Visalia Police Department officer

At almost every crime scene, police discovered the same shoe prints. The prints were from Converse All Star sneakers, size nine. People noticed these shoe prints in other yards throughout the area as well. Matching shoe prints under bedroom windows indicated that the ransacker was a peeper who routinely observed certain victims and began to stalk some of them.

Elizabeth Hupp (formerly Snelling) spoke about her encounters with the Visalia Ransacker at DeAngelo's trial. Hupp thanked her father, Claude Snelling, for saving her life.

A Failed Kidnapping

The ransacker began to watch 16-year-old Elizabeth Snelling in February 1975, or possibly earlier. Elizabeth, who went by the nickname Beth, attended Mount Whitney High School. She lived in Visalia with her mother, father, and two brothers.

At 10:00 p.m. on February 5, Beth's father, Claude Snelling, was just getting home from teaching night classes. Snelling was a journalism instructor at the College of the Sequoias. When Snelling arrived home, he saw a man at Beth's window. Snelling chased him, but it was hard to see in the dark. The man got away. The Snellings called the police. Officers found familiar shoe prints around the yard and near Beth's window. They suspected the peeper was the Visalia Ransacker.

The close encounter did not keep the ransacker away forever, and he continued to return. That summer, Beth drew back her bedroom curtains to find the ransacker looking in the window. Beth's boyfriend, who had come over to visit, also saw the ransacker. Beth's boyfriend and father rushed from the house to confront him, but again he escaped. In the following weeks, the ransacker appeared frequently near the Snellings' home, even breaking into their vehicles.

On September 10 at around 7:00 p.m., Beth was in her room when she heard a sound outside. It was already dark, and Beth did not see anyone when she checked her window. Beth went about the rest of her evening. Her boyfriend came over for a visit and left at about 10:00 p.m. Then she went to sleep for the night.

Beth had been asleep for only a few hours when she startled awake just after 2:00 a.m. The ransacker had gotten into her room and was now on top of her, covering Beth's nose and mouth with his hand. A ski mask covered his face. The man threatened to kill Beth if she screamed. He held a gun to her head and said, "You're coming with me."[5] Beth described his voice as a low, raspy growl.

The ransacker pulled Beth through the house. She struggled against him. Snelling woke up from the sound of the commotion and rushed after Beth. He shouted, "What's going on? What are you doing?"[6]

The ransacker released Beth and turned to Snelling, then shot Beth's father twice. The ransacker kicked Beth's head and face before running from the scene. Snelling died from his wounds in an ambulance on the way to the hospital. He was 45 years old.

Police found evidence of the ransacker's usual pattern when they investigated Snelling's murder. They found size nine shoe prints and a window screen the ransacker had removed from the Snellings' home. Police also discovered

COMMUNITY GRIEF

Snelling was an active member of the Visalia community as a college teacher and volunteer with the YMCA and his church. After his murder, the community honored his life and supported his family. Snelling's journalism students produced a memorial edition of the college's newspaper. The college created a scholarship named for him, and police donated money from an annual fundraiser to the scholarship. Police also walked with Beth at a high school marching band event soon after the murder to protect her. Community volunteers cleaned the Snellings' home and repaired damage from the attack.

items the ransacker had stolen to use during the attack, including a ladder and a bicycle the ransacker had ridden to the Snellings' house. Police used bullets from the crime scene to learn that DeAngelo had stolen the gun he used to murder Snelling from a nearby home on August 31.

Intensifying the Search

The ransacker continued to prowl, peep, stalk, and break into homes in Visalia after Snelling's murder. From September to December 1975, residents reported dozens more incidents. Visalia police increased patrols and organized stakeouts in an effort to capture the ransacker. They urged residents to watch for shoe prints around their homes, and the force created a special unit to oversee the investigation. Visalia police sergeant John Vaughan led this unit.

FIREARM FORENSICS

Analysis of guns and ammunition helps investigators determine the weapon used at a crime scene. Police did not find a gun at the scene of Snelling's murder, but they examined bullets from the scene. From the examination, they determined what type of gun was used. A local resident reported the same type of gun as stolen in a ransacking less than two weeks earlier. The resident took police to a location where he practiced shooting. Police compared bullets from that site to bullets from Snelling's murder. The bullets matched, and police concluded the Visalia Ransacker had used the stolen gun to kill Snelling.

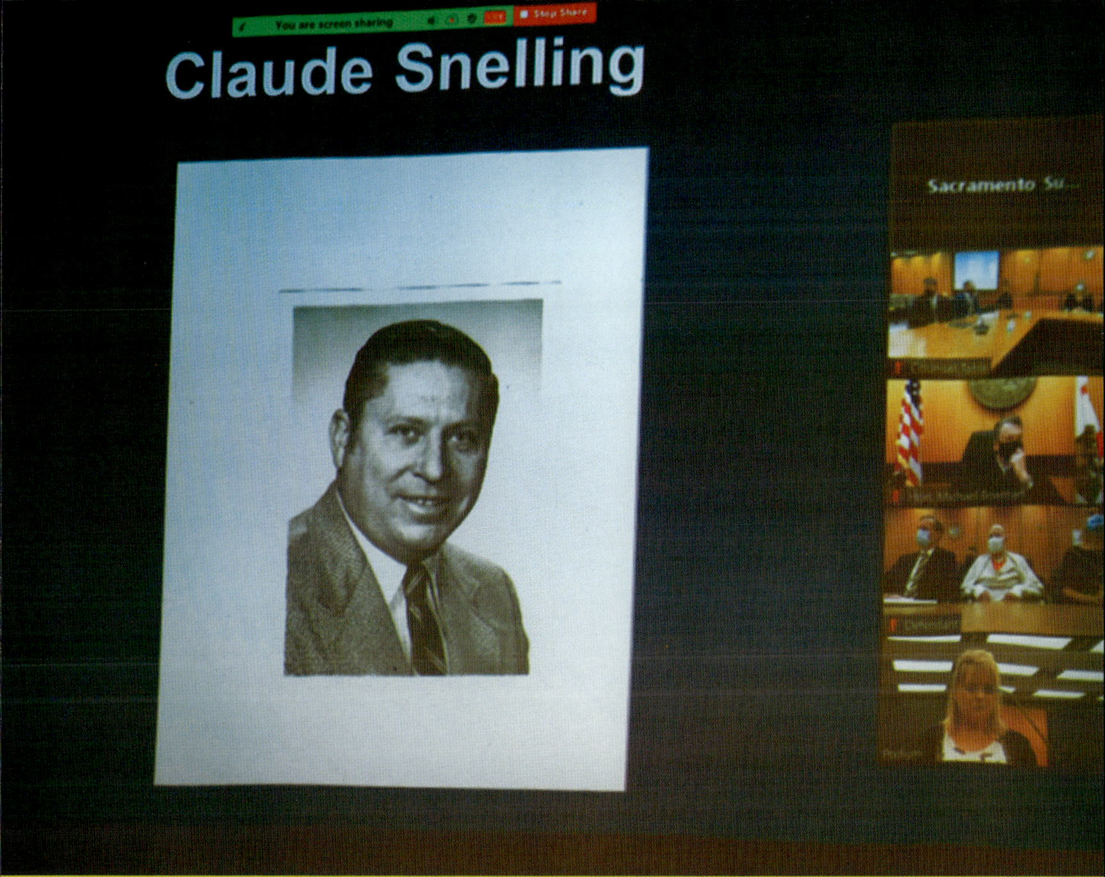

A photo was shown in memory of Claude Snelling at DeAngelo's trial.

Officers from other parts of Tulare County assisted the Visalia police in their effort. DeAngelo was among them. In the Exeter Police Department, DeAngelo was serving in the burglary unit. When assisting in Visalia, he participated in search parties looking for the Visalia Ransacker and helped canvass the area for information.

A Near Catch

On the night of December 10, 1975, two officers from Vaughan's unit were on a stakeout at a home that had reported fresh shoe prints. One of these was Officer Bill McGowen. McGowen had known Snelling personally. McGowen and his partner took up positions in different locations around the home and waited. Soon, the ransacker crept into the yard.

Detective McGowen's description of the ransacker helped the Visalia Police Department produce a sketch of the suspect in 1975.

McGowen watched the ransacker as he moved toward a gate in the backyard. McGowen approached the attacker from behind and turned on his flashlight to surprise the man. He aimed the beam at the man's head, holding his flashlight high and out to the side. McGowen could see the ransacker had a black ski cap that was rolled up on his head.

McGowen ordered the ransacker to stop. "Police officer! Hold it right there!" he said.[7] The ransacker pulled off the ski cap and began to run.

McGowen followed. He observed unusual behavior from the ransacker. He ran in circles and zigzags as if panicked. When he spoke, he used a high-pitched, squealing voice that seemed to be fake. "Please don't hurt me!" he cried.[8]

Again, McGowen ordered the ransacker to stop, but he did not. McGowen fired a warning shot into the ground. Still, the suspect continued running. He leaped over a fence into a neighboring yard. McGowen could see him through the wooden planks of the fence. The officer kept his flashlight on the ransacker and gave another order for him to put his hands up.

The ransacker raised one hand. He told McGowen that his hands were up. However, the man did not raise his other hand. Instead, he used this hand to pull a gun from his jacket and fire at McGowen.

The bullet struck McGowen's flashlight and knocked him to the ground. Debris flew from the flashlight. Some of the shards cut McGowen's face and injured his eye. Otherwise, he was unhurt. McGowen's partner rushed to help, and the ransacker fled. Although the owner of the stakeout house pursued the fleeing suspect, the ransacker got away.

The Ransacker's Disappearance

All available Visalia police responded to the area where the ransacker was spotted. Officers from the Tulare County Sheriff's Department and the California Highway Patrol also arrived. In total, almost 70 officers reported to the scene that night.[9] Nevertheless, they did not locate the ransacker.

McGowen provided details of the ransacker's face for a composite sketch. McGowen could not identify the ransacker by name, but he seemed familiar. McGowen knew he had seen him before.

The incident with McGowen was the last known crime committed by the Visalia Ransacker. The end of the ransacker's reign coincided with the end of DeAngelo's work in the Exeter Police Department. In April 1976, DeAngelo began a new job with the Auburn Police Department back in Northern California. Auburn was about 30 miles (48 km) from Rancho Cordova, where DeAngelo had grown up.

FORENSIC HYPNOSIS

Officer McGowen and Beth Snelling underwent hypnosis sessions as part of the murder investigation. Hypnosis creates a state of deep concentration in subjects. Forensic psychologists oversee hypnosis when it is used in criminal investigations. Investigators in Claude Snelling's murder hoped hypnosis could help McGowen and Beth recall details about the suspect. Some experts question the reliability of forensic hypnosis, and some states ban or limit the practice. Investigators must find additional evidence to support information revealed in a forensic hypnosis session.

CHAPTER 5

THE EAST AREA RAPIST

Two months after DeAngelo began working as an officer in Auburn, a woman in nearby Rancho Cordova called the police. It was about 5:00 a.m. on June 18, 1976. The woman, whose name was Phyllis Zitka, reported that an unknown intruder had raped her.

To make the phone call, Zitka had pushed a landline phone off a table and onto the ground. Her hands were still tied behind her back after the attack. With the phone on the ground, Zitka ran her fingers along the numbered buttons to determine which number was which and dial for help.

Zitka told police what she had observed about the attacker. He had worn gloves and a ski mask. She estimated that he was about five feet, nine inches (1.75 m) tall. He had spoken through clenched teeth in a low, growling whisper. He threatened to stab her if she moved or made noise. After he assaulted her, the attacker

Karen Veilleux spoke on behalf of her sister, Phyllis Henneman (formerly Zitka), at DeAngelo's trial. In her statement, Henneman wrote that the attack had shattered her sense of safety.

rummaged through Zitka's room and took coins, money from her purse, and a piece of jewelry. Zitka also heard him ransacking other rooms in the house.

Zitka's rape was the first of several attacks that occurred in the summer months and into the fall. In November 1976, police made a public announcement that they were looking for a serial rapist. Media and law enforcement began referring to the attacker as the East Area Rapist (EAR). The name came from the location of the crimes in eastern Sacramento County. These attacks, too, would eventually be attributed to DeAngelo.

A New Crime Spree

After the police announcement, rape attacks continued. Many of them were connected by common details. The assaults happened at night, and the EAR entered through windows or sliding glass doors. He pointed a flashlight at victims to wake them in their beds, and then he threatened to kill them with a gun or knife. He covered their eyes with towels or other blindfold material. He bound their hands and feet.

> **"Everyone was afraid. We had people sleeping with shotguns, we had people purchasing dogs. People were concerned, and they had a right to be. This guy was terrorizing the community. He did horrible things."[1]**
>
> *—Special Agent Marcus Knutson, an FBI agent who grew up in Sacramento*

The EAR wore a ski mask to hide his face and gloves to avoid leaving fingerprints. He spoke with a clenched jaw in a voice that seemed fake. Some victims described his voice as a whispering growl, and others said it was high pitched. The suspect was strong and athletic. Victims who caught glimpses of his skin said he was a white man.

During the attacks, the EAR ransacked victims' homes. He stole small items, often including coins, jewelry, and photographs. If children were present at the home, the EAR threatened violence against the children if the rape

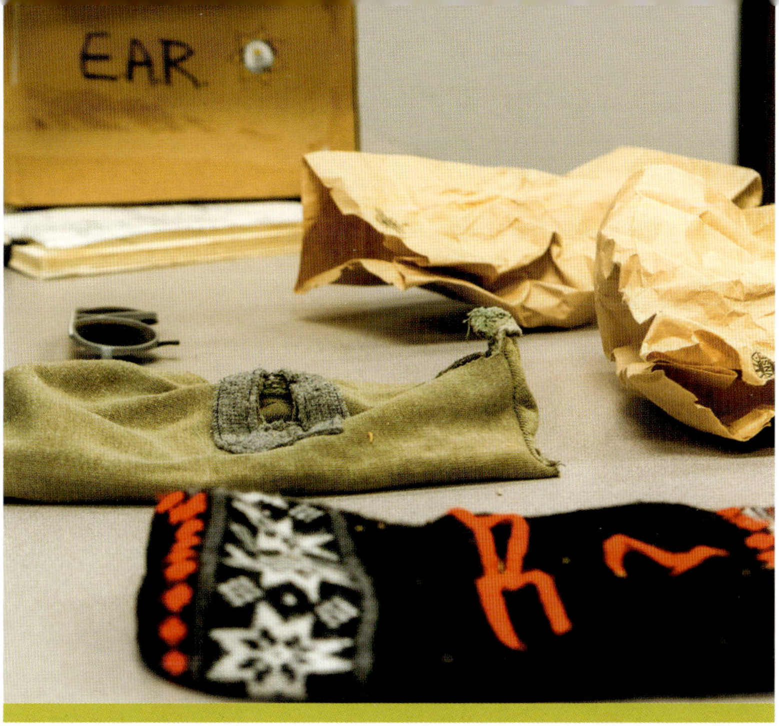

Law enforcement agencies kept several of the ski masks worn by the East Area Rapist as evidence after his attacks.

victim did not do what he said. Some of his attacks lasted for hours. Afterward, the EAR left the crime scenes on foot or by bicycle.

In March 1977, the *Sacramento Bee* newspaper printed an article about the attacks. The article observed that so far, the rapist had not committed attacks when men were home. Instead, the attacker had targeted female residents who were alone or home with children. After the *Sacramento Bee* article, the rapist also began to attack couples. Some reporters thought the change in his pattern was a direct response to the article.

When he began attacking couples, the EAR would bind them both at the hands and ankles, or he ordered women to tie up their partners. The EAR used a unique knot for the ties, which had two loops and resembled handcuffs. During each attack, he stacked dishes from the victims' kitchen on the man's back. The dishes would rattle if the man tried to break free. The attacker threatened to kill the couple if he heard rattling.

An Investigative Team

The Sacramento County Sheriff's Department created a specialized team to investigate the EAR attacks. At crime scenes, Detective Carol Daly, the only female officer on the team, took victims' statements. Investigators also searched the scenes for evidence that could help them identify a suspect. They determined the EAR wore a size nine shoe from prints he left.

> **"He knows what he's doing. He wears gloves. He conceals his identity in every way possible. His victims have limited eye contact before they're blindfolded. He disguises his voice. In fact, he disguises everything that might lead us to him."[2]**
>
> *—Detective Carol Daly*

Investigators checked for blood and other body fluids. Crime lab analysis of these fluids revealed the suspect had type A blood. The analysis also showed the EAR had an uncommon genetic trait. He was a nonsecretor, which meant his body did not secrete, or release, evidence of his blood type in other body fluids such as saliva.

This trait is so rare that it allowed police to eliminate about 98 percent of the suspects they investigated. Investigators ruled out other suspects because they had alibis or they did not match part of the EAR's description. The Sacramento EAR task force would end up eliminating about 7,000 suspects during the first two years of the attacks.[3]

A SUSPICIOUS CONNECTION

The EAR left many clues that led investigators to believe he had a law enforcement background. For instance, he shined a flashlight in victims' eyes to surprise and disorient them, which was a tactic taught in police training. Officer McGowen had used the tactic to surprise the Visalia Ransacker. In at least one attack, the rapist told a victim to freeze. Police give this order at dangerous scenes. The EAR task force believed its suspect had access to police radio communication because he changed his behavior to avoid strategies they discussed on their radios.

Two More Murders

The EAR continued his attacks as investigators worked. Attacks occurred in many Sacramento County communities, including Rancho Cordova, Citrus Heights, Carmichael, and Orangevale. By the end of January 1978, victims reported more than 20 new rape cases since police announced their search for a serial rapist in November 1976.[4]

There were also many incidents of burglaries, prowling, peeping into bedroom windows, shoe prints in yards, and suspicious phone calls. Police knew these activities were part of the EAR's pattern as he planned attacks. In January 1978, the Cordova Meadows neighborhood in Rancho Cordova reported many of these activities. Cordova Meadows was an area the EAR had struck before.

TECHNOLOGY IN THE 1970s

Police in the 1970s did not have access to the same technology available today. In a 2018 interview, Detective Daly said, "We were in the dark ages with technology when these cases first started."[5] Daly described not having GPS navigation systems, cell phones, or internet searching capabilities. Daly's husband used paper maps to help her get directions to rape scenes if she received a call at home. Homeowners did not have alarm systems with cameras, and many areas had no established 911 system.

At about 9:00 p.m. on February 2, teenager Joseph Skokan was at home in Cordova Meadows. His street was usually quiet, but that night, Joseph heard loud noises. Someone had knocked over the trash cans in his family's yard. The person crashed into one gate and broke through another. Then Joseph heard a woman screaming. He heard sounds that reminded him of firecrackers.

Joseph, his best friend who lived next door, and his best friend's father raced outside. They saw a young man on the ground. He was bleeding from a gunshot wound. Joseph's best friend's father went to the other side of the house. He found a woman who was also lying on the ground and bleeding from a gunshot wound.

Responders rushed the man and woman to a hospital, but both victims died of their wounds that night. They were newlyweds Brian and Katie Maggiore. They had been out walking their poodle when they were shot.

Police talked to Joseph, his neighbors, and other witnesses. Witnesses had seen a white man hiding in the bushes across the street from where the Maggiores were walking. The Maggiores ran through one witness's backyard with the man following them, shooting at them as they ran.

Police found a shoelace at the scene of the EAR's attack in Cordova Meadows. The shoelace was tied to create restraints similar to handcuffs.

Katie Maggiore, *left*, was 20 years old when DeAngelo murdered her. Brian Maggiore, *right*, was a 21-year-old US Air Force sergeant.

Police called to the scene were not thinking of the EAR at first. He had not killed any of his Sacramento County victims during rape attacks. However, as officers gathered evidence, they recognized details of the EAR's pattern. Police did not know why the EAR murdered the Maggiores when he had not killed other victims in the area. One idea was that the Maggiores confronted him as a suspicious person or interrupted him during a planned attack.

Changing Locations

The EAR task force publicly released a composite sketch of the suspect in April 1978. At least one witness to the Maggiores' murders had seen the EAR without his ski mask. Police used the witness's description to create the sketch.

After the sketch was released, the EAR stopped his attacks in Sacramento County. He moved to nearby areas, all within about 80 miles (129 km) of his Sacramento crimes. In June and July, the EAR raped five victims in Modesto and Davis.[6] In October, the EAR began a new series of rape attacks in Contra Costa County, which borders Sacramento County.

Victims in Contra Costa revealed familiar details of the EAR's pattern. They also shared their own stories about the EAR's frightening and unusual behavior. The EAR told one victim he had seen her many times before. He telephoned another victim a month after raping her. Some victims reported that the attacker cried. One heard him say, "I hate you, Bonnie. I hate you, I hate you, I hate you."[7] The EAR seemed to be talking about someone the victim did not know.

Contra Costa police established a task force just as Sacramento County police had. Soon a combined task force formed. Part of the investigation in Contra Costa included using sexual assault kits during victims' physical examinations. Sexual assault kits were a new investigative tool at the time. Investigators used them to collect, test, and save samples of body fluids from attackers at crime scenes.

The End of a Police Career

In June 1979, the EAR stopped his attacks in Contra Costa. By then, he had committed approximately 45 known rape attacks in total.[8] His youngest known victims were 13 years old. The oldest was 41.

The EAR attacks ended at about the same time that DeAngelo lost his job at the Auburn Police Department. In early July, a clerk at a convenience store caught DeAngelo stealing a can of dog repellant and a hammer. Nick Willick, the Auburn police chief, fired DeAngelo, but he did not suspect him of the more serious EAR crimes.

A VISIT FROM THE EAST AREA RAPIST

After Police Chief Willick fired DeAngelo, Willick's daughter told him she saw a man looking through her window with a flashlight one night. DeAngelo confessed the incident to a therapist soon after it happened. DeAngelo had filed a lawsuit against the city of Auburn, claiming he suffered mental distress when Willick fired him. Seeing a therapist was a requirement while the city looked into the lawsuit. DeAngelo told the therapist he was trying to find Willick's bedroom window because he wanted to kill Willick.

FORENSIC SPOTLIGHT
Sexual Assault Kits

Doctors and other medical professionals use sexual assault kits to collect and preserve forensic evidence for criminal investigations. The evidence may include hair or body fluids left by an attacker on a victim's body. Sexual assault kits were developed in Chicago, Illinois, in the 1970s. Martha Goddard got the idea from her work with an advocacy group for victims of sexual assault and researched a design for them.

Sexual assault kits contain a comb to gather evidence left in the victim's hair, nail clippers to gather evidence from under their fingernails, and cotton swabs to gather evidence from other parts of the victim's body. Glass slides, plastic test tubes, and labeled envelopes in the kit preserve the evidence samples. There is a paper bag for storing the victim's clothing as evidence. There is also a checklist of steps for completing the kit and forms for medical staff, police, and the victim to fill out. One compact cardboard box holds all the kit's items. Medical professionals throughout the United States still use these kits.

Sexual assault kits include a variety of tools for collecting evidence.

In 1978, Chicago hospitals began to use sexual assault kits. Soon more hospitals in Illinois and other states also began to use them. Sexual assault kits collected by medical professionals in three EAR attacks and three later attacks provided the key evidence in connecting the crimes and ultimately identifying the killer.

CHAPTER 6

THE ORIGINAL NIGHT STALKER

Stan Los, a special agent in the Federal Bureau of Investigation (FBI), woke suddenly in the middle of the night on October 1, 1979. It was after 2:00 a.m. A woman who lived next door was screaming. Crime was not common in Los's upper-middle-class neighborhood.

Los took action as soon as he woke. He looked out the window, but bushes blocked the view of the neighbors' house. His neighbors, Jennifer Horinek and Abraham Himmel, were 33 years old and worked as computer programmers. Los called the county sheriff's department, got his gun, and went outside to investigate. As he left, he told his wife to lock the door behind him and not open it until he returned.

Outside, Los saw a man bicycling away from his neighbors' house. Los got into his car and followed, but the man escaped. Los drove back to his neighbors' house, where an officer had just arrived. Horinek and

When officers from the sheriff's department arrived at Horinek and Himmel's house, they found details of the attack that matched those from EAR crime scenes.

Himmel told Los and the officer what had happened. A man in a ski mask had entered their bedroom. He shined a flashlight at them and ordered Horinek to tie Himmel's wrists and ankles. Then the man tied Horinek's wrists and ankles. He seemed to speak in a fake voice—a growling whisper—while he gave orders.

The intruder left Himmel in the bedroom. He brought Horinek into the living room and threatened to kill her with a knife. He left her there while he rummaged through the kitchen. She heard him say, "I'm going to kill them this time."[1] Horinek took the opportunity to move her ankles and loosen the ties.

She ran out the front door and screamed. She could not see well because the man had covered her head with a pair of her athletic shorts. He soon caught her and forced her back into the house. Himmel heard the screams. His ankles were still tied, but he hopped through the bedroom's sliding glass door into the backyard. Police found both Horinek and Himmel soon after the attacker fled.

Law enforcement kept track of the locations where similar crimes had occurred. The patterns would later help detectives identify the perpetrator of these connected crimes.

The Beginning of a Murder Series

The attack against Himmel and Horinek followed a pattern similar to the EAR's, but it occurred in a region of California that the EAR had never struck. Goleta was more than 300 miles (480 km) south of Contra Costa, where the EAR's last attack occurred on June 25, 1979. In Southern California, the attacker became known as the Night Stalker because the intrusions took place at night or in the early morning hours when it was dark outside.

In the mid-1980s, a different serial killer, Richard Ramirez, was also named the Night Stalker. The man who attacked Himmel and Horinek became known as the Original Night Stalker (ONS). Many years later, police discovered that this man was DeAngelo.

Los's neighbors were able to interrupt the first of the ONS's attacks. Almost three months later, a second occurred. Early in the morning on December 30, 1979, the ONS trespassed into Robert Offerman's backyard by climbing over a fence. Offerman lived in a condominium in Goleta. His girlfriend, Debra Manning, was staying with him that weekend.

Once inside Offerman's yard, the ONS looked through one of the condominium's windows and saw Offerman and Manning sleeping. He pried open a sliding glass door and went into their bedroom. He tied Manning's wrists and raped her.

Offerman's wrists were also tied, but he managed to free himself and tried to tackle the ONS. The ONS bludgeoned him and shot him, then shot Manning. Later that morning, two friends of Offerman and Manning arrived at the condominium and discovered their bodies.

The Ventura County Murders

Two and a half months later, the ONS broke into Charlene and Lyman Smith's house at night on March 13, 1980. The Smiths lived in Ventura County, which is just south of Santa Barbara County. Lyman was the district attorney in Ventura County. Many people thought California's governor would appoint him as a judge soon. Charlene worked as a legal secretary before she and Lyman married.

The ONS left no sign of how he entered the house. Once inside, he went to the couple's bedroom. He tied Lyman's wrists and ankles, or he made Charlene tie them. After that, the ONS tied Charlene's wrists and ankles and raped her.

The ONS did not shoot the Smiths. He took a log from a pile of firewood in the house to use as a weapon.

He bludgeoned Lyman and Charlene with the log, and they died from head injuries.

On the afternoon of March 16, Lyman's son, Gary, went to the Smiths' house. He discovered Lyman and Charlene's bodies and called the police. Law enforcement found the log used in the murder on the bed near the Smiths' bodies. A medical examiner also responded to the scene. The medical examiner completed a sexual assault kit and preserved samples of body fluids left by the attacker.

AN ARREST

A large investigation took place after the Smiths' murders. Ventura County police and the FBI collaborated. In November 1981, investigators arrested Joseph Alsip Jr., one of Lyman's colleagues. Alsip had been to the Smiths' home before their murders. Police found Alsip's fingerprints on a glass in the Smiths' kitchen. In addition, someone had come to the police with statements against him. Prosecutors dropped the case when they learned the statements were not credible.

The Orange County Murders

Five months passed after the Smiths' murders. Then the ONS broke into Keith and Patrice Harrington's house on August 19, 1980. Their house was in Dana Point in Orange County. Orange County is to the south of Ventura County, past Los Angeles County.

The Harringtons had celebrated their wedding just three months earlier. Patrice, called Patti by her family, was

PETER SPETH

Peter Speth was the medical examiner assigned to the Smiths' murder case. Medical examiners often wait to perform an exam until police transport the body to the crime lab, but Speth preferred to travel to crime scenes. Speth took two samples of body fluids left by the ONS on Charlene Smith's body. One was for investigators to use at the time. Speth sealed the other for investigators to use later, in case new technology became available. Collecting two samples was not common practice. However, this second sample was eventually pivotal in identifying the ONS.

27 and a pediatric nurse. Keith was 24 and finishing his last year of medical school at the University of California, Irvine.

After breaking into the Harringtons' house, the ONS followed a similar pattern to the Smiths' murders. He bound Keith and Patrice. He raped Patrice and bludgeoned her. He also bludgeoned Keith. The Harringtons died from head trauma caused by the bludgeoning.

Keith's father, Roger Harrington, went to the home at about 6:30 p.m. on August 21. There was no immediate sign of a break-in, but Roger found the Harringtons' bodies as soon as he got to the bedroom. Investigators used a sexual assault kit to take samples of body fluids left on Patrice's body.

Almost six months later, on February 5, 1981, 28-year-old Manuela Witthuhn returned home alone after visiting her husband, David, in the hospital. David had been in the hospital for several days recovering from an illness. Similar to the Harringtons, the Witthuhns lived in Orange County. Manuela spoke to David on the telephone when she got home and then went to sleep.

The ONS used a screwdriver to pry open a sliding glass door of the home. He left the screwdriver on the patio near the door and went inside. He attacked Manuela in her bed, tying her wrists and ankles before raping her. He took a heavy lamp from the bedside and bludgeoned her. Manuela died from head injuries.

David called Manuela's father in the morning on February 6. David had not been able to get in touch with

Bruce Harrington, Keith Harrington's brother, spoke to the media about Keith and Patrice's murders. He pushed for new investigative methods to identify his brother's killer.

his wife that morning. Manuela's mother checked on the house and discovered her body.

When police investigated, they found shoe prints around the Witthuhns' yard and damage to a fence in the backyard. The damage showed someone had climbed the fence. Investigators used a sexual assault kit to take samples of body fluids left on Manuela's body.

Returning to Goleta

The ONS returned to Goleta in July 1981. On the night of July 26, 35-year-old Cheri Domingo was at her aunt's home. Domingo's aunt had moved and asked Domingo to house-sit the property while she tried to sell it. Domingo's boyfriend, Greg Sanchez, was also at the home that night. Her two teenage children, David and Debbi, were not there.

THE TOLL ON FAMILIES

Manuela Witthuhn's parents were from Germany. Manuela was their only child. They returned to Germany soon after their daughter's murder. They were too distraught to say goodbye or keep in touch with David's family. They died a few years later, and David remarried. The ONS continued to call David and his second wife with threatening messages. The calls forced them to move. David died in 2008. His brother, Drew, said the effects of the ONS attack contributed to his death. David had suffered from grief, anxiety, and depression ever since Witthuhn's murder.

Melanie Barbeau, a social worker involved in the case, held a photo of Cheri Domingo and Greg Sanchez at DeAngelo's trial.

The ONS removed a screen from one of the home's small windows. He reached through the window, unlocked a door, and went inside to the bedroom where Domingo and Sanchez were sleeping. The ONS shot the man in the cheek, but the wound was not fatal. Sanchez got out of bed and struggled with the attacker. The ONS then used a hard, blunt object to bludgeon Sanchez's head. Sanchez died from his head injuries.

Domingo spoke to the ONS, urging him to calm down. The ONS tied her wrists and ankles and raped her. He bludgeoned her with the same object he used to bludgeon Sanchez. Domingo also died from head injuries.

One of the tools missing from the Sanchez and Domingo crime scene was a pipe wrench. Pipe wrenches were suspected murder weapons in other cases later connected to DeAngelo.

The ONS threw clothes from the closet over Sanchez's body and took a pair of pants to change into. He removed the ligatures from Domingo's wrists and took them with him. The ligatures left marks on her body. There were no ligature marks on Sanchez's wrists or ankles.

Later in the morning on July 27, a real estate agent arrived at the house to show it to a client. He discovered the murders and called the police. At the scene, police did not find the murder weapon. However, they discovered tools missing from the home and believed the ONS used one to bludgeon his victims before taking it with him. Police also discovered a flashlight at the scene.

The End of a Crime Spree

Domingo's and Sanchez's murders were the last ONS attacks for five years. Then, in May 1986, the ONS returned to Orange County for the attack that killed Janelle Cruz in Irvine. With Cruz's murder, the ONS had killed ten people in three Southern California counties.[2] After that, he never committed another known murder.

DeAngelo never raised suspicion as the ONS. He continued to lead his double life, and he and his wife started a family. Their first daughter was born in 1981 in Sacramento. They had a second daughter in 1986, and a third daughter was born in 1989.

CHAPTER 7

COLD CASES

Investigators from the different Southern California towns where the ONS struck debated whether the murders were the work of one serial killer or different people. Police considered similarities in the attacks, but there were also differences. For example, Offerman and Manning died of gunshot wounds, but other victims died from bludgeoning. Some of the victims were couples, but some were women alone. In addition, the murders had not all happened in the same county, and there were other California serial killers committing crimes similar to the ONS's.

Although detectives lifted some fingerprints from EAR and ONS crime scenes, they could not match the fingerprints in order to identify the criminal.

2ND LIFT

As Southern California police investigated, police from the EAR task force in Northern California learned about the ONS killings. They contacted Southern California investigators to point out similarities in the crime patterns. Sergeant Larry Crompton, a Contra Costa County officer, said, "It is our man. No doubt about it."[1] Southern California police were uncertain about the connection. Without conclusive evidence, it was difficult for law enforcement to link the various crimes.

Eventually, the ONS cases grew cold, as did the EAR and Visalia Ransacker cases. Police refer to cases as *cold* once officers have used all available investigative tools and followed all leads without identifying the perpetrator. Cold cases can reopen when new technology or leads develop.

A DNA Breakthrough

In 1996, Mary Hong worked in the Orange County Sheriff's Department crime lab. The department had recently formed a cold case unit. The cold case unit reexamined old cases using newly developed DNA technology, which allowed investigators to see patterns in a sample of DNA. These patterns are called DNA profiles. If two samples have identical patterns, it means they came from the same person. Investigators could prove that one perpetrator committed several crimes if the DNA from all the crime scenes had matching profiles. Hong applied this technology to samples taken from the ONS murders in Orange County.

Hong discovered matching DNA profiles from all the Orange County cases: the murders of Janelle Cruz, Manuela Witthuhn, and Keith and Patrice Harrington. The matching DNA profiles were conclusive evidence that the same person committed each of those murders. By 2000, investigators had matched these profiles to a DNA profile from evidence taken at the scene of Charlene and Lyman Smith's murders in Ventura County.

"The big problem is we don't know whose DNA it is. But a greater database is being built daily, so I hope this one will be solved."[2]

—Michael Bradbury, district attorney in Ventura County in 2000

Investigators also looked into a connection with the ONS murders in Santa Barbara County. These were the murders of Debra Manning, Robert Offerman, Cheri Domingo, and Gregory Sanchez. However, there were no DNA samples to test from those cases at the time.

Investigators still did not know who that killer was. To identify the killer by name, they needed to find a match for his DNA profile. Investigators could collect a sample from a suspect and create a DNA profile. Next, they could compare the suspect's profile to the ONS's profile. If the profiles matched, it would mean the suspect was the ONS. But investigators did not yet have a suspect.

Building Connections

Paul Holes, a Contra Costa cold case investigator, had been a child during the ONS and EAR attacks. He learned about the EAR crimes in 1994, when he found case files in a police library. In 1997, Holes discovered Contra Costa police had three sexual assault kits from EAR attacks in storage. Holes used these samples to produce a DNA profile of the EAR.

Holes discussed his work with Larry Crompton, an original EAR task force officer. Holes then called Detective Larry Montgomery, an original officer on the ONS cases.

ANOTHER DNA MATCH

As DNA technology advanced, Santa Barbara investigators reexamined the pieces of evidence they had collected. In the murders of Domingo and Sanchez, investigators looked at more than 50 items.[3] One of the items was a blanket with a stain of body fluids from the ONS. A crime lab was able to obtain DNA from the stain and produce a DNA profile. The profile matched those of the ONS murders in Ventura and Orange Counties.

Montgomery had investigated the Witthuhn and Cruz murders in Orange County.

Holes heard about Hong's DNA work from Montgomery, but at the time, Contra Costa County authorities did not have the advanced technology necessary to compare Holes's profile of the EAR with that of the ONS. Four years later, in 2001, Contra Costa County acquired the necessary equipment. This allowed Holes and Hong to compare the DNA of the EAR and the ONS.

Their DNA profiles matched, which provided conclusive evidence that the EAR and the ONS were the same person. Police began referring to the attacker as EARONS. Nevertheless, investigators still did not have a suspect who fit the DNA profile.

Dedicated Networks

As technology evolved, a new task force formed, and its members collaborated with officers who had worked the original EARONS cases. Detective Daly from the original EAR task force in Sacramento kept in touch with victims and told them, "It's called a cold case, but . . . it [has] never been forgotten."[4]

Bill McGowen, the officer who confronted the Visalia Ransacker during a 1975 stakeout, also continued to work

TAUNTING POLICE

During the 1970s, the EARONS had telephoned police stations to taunt officers. On the phone, he identified himself as the attacker but did not provide his name. He insulted officers' investigative work and called them names. Some days he called to tell police that he would commit another attack that same night. Into the 2000s, the EARONS continued calling his previous victims. He sometimes said insulting things about the police on these calls.

on the cases in retirement. When the EAR attacks began in Northern California, McGowen and other Visalia officers tried to persuade the EAR task force to look into connections with the Visalia Ransacker. The task force dismissed the connection. However, McGowen never gave up on the idea that they were the same person.

McGowen retired in 1985, but he still assisted other officers who contacted him about the case. McGowen's son, Brett, said, "He wanted to solve it, and I'm sure most of the detectives around here would say the same thing."[5] McGowen's daughter said he followed up on every new possible suspect.

Victims' family members also remained dedicated to identifying the EARONS. Several became active in research and advocacy. For instance, Keith Harrington's brothers, Ron, Bruce, and Doug, advocated for advancements in DNA testing and databases.

Janelle Cruz's sister Michelle Cruz earned a criminal justice degree and researched the case in her free time.

FORENSIC SPOTLIGHT

DNA Testing

DNA is a molecule that contains a person's genetic information. Each person has a unique sequence of genes in their DNA. DNA is present in samples taken from body fluids, skin cells, hair, bone, fingernails, and other parts of the body.

There are multiple ways to create a DNA profile. When forensic DNA technology was still relatively new, there was not a standard system to ensure that labs used the same type of DNA tests. Without using the same technique, labs could not determine if two profiles matched.

In Contra Costa County, the crime lab used a basic technique that created a profile based on the presence of a gene called DQ alpha. In Orange County, crime labs created a DNA profile of the ONS using a different technique that looked for short tandem repeats, or STRs, in DNA. STR technology finds places where the sequence of genes repeats in DNA. This type of DNA profile is more accurate than DQ alpha, and it remains the standard for law enforcement today.

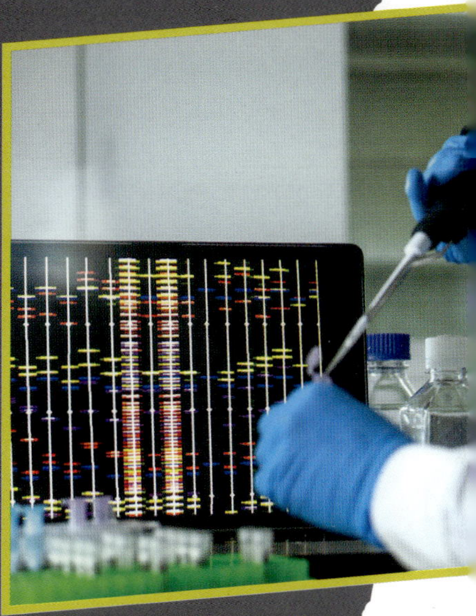

Scientists may use charts or visual illustrations to show a DNA sequence. These images can help show patterns in DNA profiles.

It would not be until 2001 that Contra Costa County gained access to the more advanced STR technology. Finally, Contra Costa could compare its DNA profile to Orange County's. The comparison gave investigators the evidence necessary to prove one suspect was responsible for both crime sprees.

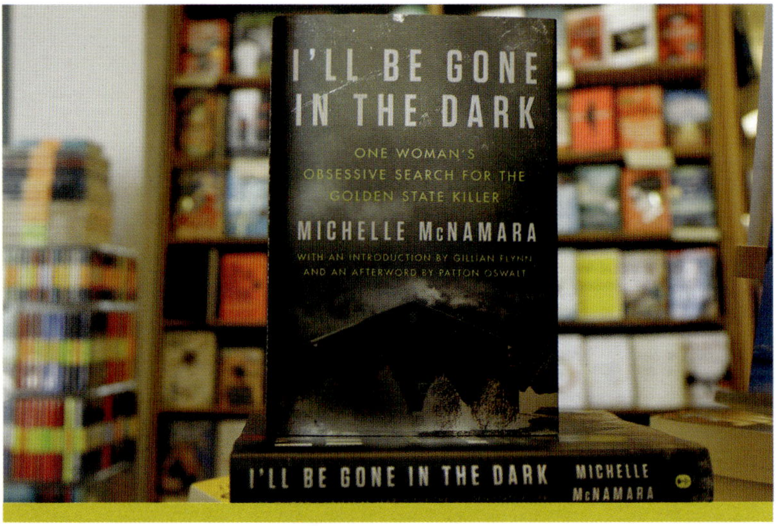

Michelle McNamara eventually wrote a book about her amateur investigation into the EARONS case, called *I'll Be Gone in the Dark*.

Cruz did interviews to bring awareness to the case. She connected with survivors from the Northern California rapes and other family members from the Southern California murders.

Cruz also connected with amateur detectives through an online message board. Amateur detectives are people who have an interest in crime investigations but do not work in law enforcement. Cruz's connections shared research, tips, and leads. Cheri Domingo's daughter Debbi also connected online with amateur detectives. She praised the internet community for helping keep attention on the case.

Writer Michelle McNamara was one of the amateur detectives active in the internet community surrounding EARONS. In 2006, McNamara began writing the blog

True Crime Diary. She started to focus on the EARONS cases. In February 2013, McNamara wrote an article for *Los Angeles Magazine* referring to the EARONS by a new name: the Golden State Killer. California is nicknamed the Golden State. Referring to the attacker as the Golden State Killer reflected the fact that he had committed crimes in so many parts of the state. Police and media adopted the name.

In June 2016, the FBI and California police launched a national campaign in hopes of gaining new leads from the public. They created a web page about the Golden State Killer's crimes and encouraged people to share any information they had. They offered a $50,000 reward for information that could help them identify, arrest, and convict the killer.[6]

WHERE WAS THE GOLDEN STATE KILLER?

Many ideas developed about the killer's whereabouts in the years following his last known attack in 1986. Some people thought the killer had been captured for a different crime and was in prison. Others believed he had died. Another thought was that the killer had grown too old to commit further crimes. Evidence and statements from victims and witnesses showed the killer's crimes had required force and physical strength. Others believed the killer could still be living free in society. He could be drifting from place to place or leading a quiet life with his family.

CHAPTER 8

CATCHING THE KILLER

By 2017, more than 40 years had passed since the Golden State Killer's crimes began. Fifteen law enforcement agencies had been involved in the investigation throughout that time.[1] Police knew they were looking for one man who was a serial killer and rapist. However, the DNA technology so far could not lead them to a suspect.

In early 2017, Steve Kramer learned about a new approach with DNA technology that had solved a different cold case. Kramer worked as an attorney for the FBI. He became

At crime scenes, law enforcement officers should wear gloves and a face mask when collecting DNA samples so evidence is not contaminated.

SANTA ANA
POLICE

involved in the Golden State Killer case after reading McNamara's 2013 *Los Angeles Magazine* article.

Researchers and investigators referred to the new DNA approach as investigative genetic genealogy, or simply genetic genealogy. Genealogy is the practice of creating family trees that list people's relatives and ancestors. Kramer contacted investigator Holes to tell him what he had learned about genetic genealogy. They believed it could help identify the Golden State Killer.

Genealogy Research

Holes reached out to Barbara Rae-Venter. Rae-Venter had led the research in a previous cold case that had been solved with genetic genealogy. Rae-Venter began working in genetic genealogy after retiring from her career as a lawyer. She also had a PhD in biology. Rae-Venter agreed to assist with the Golden State Killer case and started work in late 2017.

Rae-Venter was not allowed to see previous DNA profiles from the Golden State Killer. Only law enforcement professionals had access to those files. Rae-Venter needed to run a new test to get the Golden State Killer's DNA profile, which required a sample of his DNA from a crime scene. However, police had used many of the samples in previous DNA tests. Holes and Kramer contacted various California police departments to try to locate a usable sample.

Meanwhile, Rae-Venter studied known facts about the Golden State Killer to guide her research. Rae-Venter knew they were looking for a man who had lived in California. Survivor and witness statements described him as a white man with blond or light brown hair and an approximate height of five feet, ten inches (1.78 m). Rae-Venter estimated that the attacker was born in the mid-1950s or earlier, based on the years when the crimes took place.

In November 2017, Holes told Rae-Venter they had found an unused DNA sample from Charlene Smith's sexual assault kit in Ventura County. A private company created a DNA profile from the sample using a new, more advanced form of testing. The company provided its DNA testing services

THE KILLER'S APPEARANCE

Documents for DeAngelo's arrest confirmed many previous descriptions of the Golden State Killer. An official document reported DeAngelo as a white man with blue eyes. He was five feet, 11 inches (1.80 m) tall and 200 pounds (91 kg). The document identified his hair color as brown, but it was gray by the time he was arrested. These details matched victims' and witnesses' accounts of the Golden State Killer. Witnesses also described him as having a round face. Decades later, a neighbor described his face in the same way.

Time magazine honored Barbara Rae-Venter on the 2019 Time100 list of Most Influential People for her work on the Golden State Killer case.

to people who wanted to learn about their ancestry. The company had an online database of DNA profiles from people who used its service.

Rae-Venter waited for that company and another private genealogy company to do an analysis. The analysis compared the Golden State Killer's DNA profile to other DNA profiles in their databases. It checked for biological relatives who had submitted their DNA samples for ancestry testing.

Biological relatives have DNA in common. Researchers can determine the relationship between two biological relatives based on how much identical DNA they share.

First cousins have about 12 percent of their DNA in common. Second cousins share about 3 percent.[2]

Rae-Venter hoped the analysis would find a second cousin or an even closer relative to the Golden State Killer. Rae-Venter could then use that relative as a starting point to build a family tree. From there, she could look for individuals who matched the known facts about the killer outlined in her initial profile.

While waiting for the analysis results, Rae-Venter used other tools on the genealogy websites. The tools made additional predictions about the Golden State Killer's appearance based on his DNA profile. The tools could make predictions because genes in DNA determine what a person looks like. For example, genes determine height, eye color, and natural hair color. The website tools Rae-Venter used predicted that the Golden State Killer had blue eyes based on his genes.

A Match

Analysis results from the two genealogy companies did not produce close relative matches for the Golden State Killer's DNA profile. Rae-Venter then uploaded the profile to another company's website. That website compared the profile to its database and found a second-cousin match.

Rae-Venter and a research team used that match to build a family tree. They identified relatives of the second cousin using public records, including birth certificates, marriage licenses, death certificates, grave site information, and census data.

> **"Finding a second-cousin match to the Golden State Killer was a breakthrough moment. There was still a lot of work to be done, but it seemed not only doable, but also something we could do fairly quickly."[4]**
>
> *—Barbara Rae-Venter, genetic genealogist*

Rae-Venter continued to use features on the genealogy websites to sort through the family tree. She discovered nine men on the family tree who fit the details she had deduced of the Golden State Killer, such as his likely age and the fact that he had lived in California.

Holes obtained a DNA sample from a woman closely related to one of the men on the list. The DNA revealed the Golden State Killer had to be related to the woman on his mother's side, not his father's. That information helped shorten the list from nine men to six.[3]

In late March 2018, Rae-Venter used the eye-color prediction to shorten the list even more. She asked Holes and Kramer to contact the California Department of Motor Vehicles for driver's license records of the six men.

Those records showed eye color as well as birth years, height, and weight. The records included just one man with blue eyes: Joseph James DeAngelo.

The investigative team had uncovered additional research from news articles and old case files that supported DeAngelo as a suspect. They found a 1979 article about DeAngelo's firing from the Auburn Police Department because he had stolen a can of dog repellant and a hammer. Holes followed up on this information with a visit to Nick Willick, the police chief who had fired DeAngelo. Willick told him that he believed DeAngelo had prowled around the family's home and looked into windows with a flashlight soon after being fired.

AN ARREST IN THE 1990s

DeAngelo had one previous arrest in Sacramento County. On July 28, 1995, DeAngelo went to a gas station. He said he prepaid for gas, but the pump malfunctioned before he received the amount of gas he had paid for. When DeAngelo went inside to ask for a refund, the clerk didn't understand him, so DeAngelo left. The clerk reported him for attempted robbery. DeAngelo said the incident was a misunderstanding. Later, police processed DeAngelo's arrest at a county jail, where he spent about three hours. Police then released him, and the case was dismissed. At that time, it was not standard procedure to take DNA samples when first processing an arrest.

The team also learned that DeAngelo had been engaged to a woman named Bonnie Colwell. This detail raised suspicion when compared to a case file from a 1978 EAR attack, where the victim heard the EAR say, "I hate you, Bonnie."[5] Police contacted Colwell. She told them about DeAngelo's appearance at her window with a gun one night after their breakup.

The DNA evidence and the details about DeAngelo's life were enough to persuade the police to proceed with their investigation of DeAngelo. Now they needed to locate DeAngelo and obtain a sample of his DNA without him knowing. Police would have conclusive evidence that DeAngelo was the Golden State Killer if his DNA was a definite match to the crime scene DNA.

Undercover Surveillance

Police identified DeAngelo's home address in Citrus Heights, a city where several EAR attacks in the late 1970s took place. DeAngelo's home was a single-story ranch-style house in a quiet neighborhood where DeAngelo had lived for decades. His oldest daughter and his 15-year-old granddaughter lived with him.

In the middle of April 2018, FBI agents and police from the Sacramento County Sheriff's Department worked undercover to observe the home and follow DeAngelo. They watched for an opportunity to obtain the DNA sample they needed. The sample could come from an object DeAngelo touched, used, or ate or drank from.

As they waited for an opportunity, officers observed DeAngelo going about his day-to-day life. He did yard work, keeping the front lawn tidy. DeAngelo was 72 years old, but he was still able to lift heavy items while he worked. He had a fishing boat and a motorcycle in addition to his other vehicles. Officers observed him driving the motorcycle at 100 miles per hour (160 kmh).[6]

On April 18, police followed as DeAngelo drove another of his vehicles to Hobby Lobby. They swabbed the car's door handle for DNA while he was in the store. Test results showed the sample matched the DNA profile of the Golden State Killer.

Sacramento's district attorney, Anne Marie Schubert, requested a second sample. Schubert wanted the

THE CITRUS HEIGHTS HOME

DeAngelo began living at the house in Citrus Heights in 1983. He moved to Southern California for a time and then returned to the house. After DeAngelo's arrest, police processed the home for evidence of his crimes. Police then released the home back to DeAngelo's family members, who sold the home privately in 2019. The sale price was low compared with other sales for similar homes in the area.

Police eventually searched DeAngelo's home. Paul Holes said that details inside the house reminded him of crime scenes from the Golden State Killer's attacks.

additional evidence because it was such an important case. Officers obtained the second sample from a tissue DeAngelo discarded into a trash can on April 23. DeAngelo had left the trash can in his front yard for garbage collection.

The next day, April 24, DNA test results showed the second sample also matched the DNA of the Golden State Killer. Ken Clark, a detective in the Sacramento County Sheriff's Department, submitted a document requesting the arrest warrant that same day. The request document mentioned the Visalia Ransacker, EAR, and ONS cases. Police did not have DNA evidence from the Visalia Ransacker cases. They based the connection on other evidence and similarities with the EAR and ONS cases. The warrant was issued.

Police arrested DeAngelo in the yard of his home on April 24, 2018. He did not resist arrest. The only thing he said was, "I have a roast in the oven. . . . Cooking."[7] The arresting officers said they would take care of it.

CHAPTER 9

SENTENCED FOR LIFE

DeAngelo did not speak to investigators after his arrest. He sat motionless in the interrogation room and looked at the wall. Investigators left him alone in the room, but they had the ability to watch him and listen to anything he might say. DeAngelo began to speak to himself in the empty room. He said some things investigators did not understand. Then he said, "I did all those things. I've destroyed all their lives. So now I got to pay the price."[1]

Pleading Guilty

On June 29, 2020, DeAngelo entered a guilty plea as part of an agreement that removed the death penalty as a sentencing option. DeAngelo pleaded guilty to 13 counts of first-degree murder and 13 rape-related charges.[2] The murder charges included the deaths of all ten victims in the Southern California attacks, Claude Snelling's

A few days after DeAngelo was arrested, he appeared in court for his arraignment hearing. This initial hearing is when a judge informs the defendant about the charges against him.

death in Visalia, and Katie and Brian Maggiore's deaths in Rancho Cordova.

Many of the other rape attacks DeAngelo had committed were past the statute of limitations. A statute of limitations is the amount of time prosecutors have to begin legal actions for a crime. The amount of time depends on the crime and the state where it took place.

In California, the statute of limitations for rape was ten years when DeAngelo's attacks occurred. This statute of

DeAngelo's defense team included public defenders Diane Howard, *right*, and Joe Cress, *left*.

limitations applied only if the rape victim survived. There was no statute of limitations if the person was murdered.

Prosecutors could not charge DeAngelo with crimes past the statute of limitations, but they acknowledged those crimes at his court hearing. They also acknowledged another uncharged crime, the attempted murder of Officer McGowen. This uncharged crime came from the confrontation when DeAngelo shot at Officer McGowen during his crime spree as the Visalia Ransacker.

Judge Michael Bowman asked, "Do you admit or deny [the attempted murder]?" DeAngelo replied, "I admit."[3] He also admitted to dozens of uncharged rapes.

Life in Prison

On August 21, 2020, Judge Bowman sentenced DeAngelo to 11 consecutive life terms in prison.[4] The sentence ensured he would remain in prison until his death. Judge Bowman expressed his hope that the sentence would bring closure for the survivors of DeAngelo's crimes.

"I'm forever grateful to all those involved in making it possible to bring [DeAngelo] to justice, so he can be held accountable for all of these crimes, even those outside the statute of limitations."[5]

–Mary Berwert, a survivor from Contra Costa County

The sentencing hearing took place in a ballroom at California State University, Sacramento, providing enough room for the large number of victims and their family members and friends who attended. DeAngelo had graduated from the same university 46 years earlier with a criminal justice degree to begin his police career. As prosecutors read the details of the attacks, many of the survivors stood up and remained standing to show their support for one another.

Several survivors, family members, and friends gave victim impact statements in the sentencing hearing. Beth Hupp described the night her father was murdered. She called her father a hero. A husband who was tied while DeAngelo sexually assaulted his wife mentioned nightmares, grief, and guilt about not being able to protect his wife. He said their family was never the same.

Katie Maggiore's brother, Ken Smith, said he would remember Katie and Brian for the rest of his life. Another survivor, who was 23 when DeAngelo raped her, said to him, "You will not defeat me, you will not break me."[6] Some victims chose not to give statements. According to a news report, they said he was not worth their time or words.

POLICE REACTIONS

One survivor, Gay Hardwick, said, "What a gut punch it was that I had been brutally raped by a full-time police officer. To learn that DeAngelo, who was sworn to serve and protect, used his skill set to terrorize and rape."[7] Police reacted to DeAngelo's arrest and sentencing with relief. They also felt embarrassed. Officer Willick, who had been DeAngelo's police chief in Auburn, said DeAngelo's crimes reflected poorly on his department and law enforcement generally. Some victims expressed frustration that police had not suspected DeAngelo. Police said some of the clues about DeAngelo's double life fit in hindsight but did not raise alarm at the time.

DeAngelo also gave a statement at the sentencing. In the statement, he apologized for his crimes. He said, "I've

More than 100 people attended DeAngelo's trial. They sat spaced apart as a precaution during the COVID-19 pandemic. The hearing was also live streamed for those who could not attend.

listened to all your statements. Each one of them. And I'm truly sorry to everyone I've hurt."[8] The statement was only a few seconds long, and many survivors dismissed it. They did not believe DeAngelo showed sincere remorse.

Unanswered Questions

DeAngelo did not provide a motive for his attacks when he gave his apology. However, victims, investigators, prosecutors, and other experts developed theories to explain DeAngelo's crimes. One theory was that witnessing and experiencing abuse as a child could have contributed to his violent behavior. Another theory was that his broken engagement with Colwell caused DeAngelo to have anger toward women, and he acted on that anger in a violent way.

MOVING ON

Bonnie Colwell married her husband in August 1972 before her senior year at California State University, Sacramento. She took her husband's last name, Ueltzen, and the couple lived in Sacramento. Later in life, she and her husband divorced, and Bonnie spent time traveling outside the United States. When Bonnie was contacted about DeAngelo in 2018, she was living in Italy. Bonnie accompanied Jane Carson-Sandler, a rape attack survivor, to court. Carson-Sandler told DeAngelo, "[Bonnie] bears none of that responsibility of your violent choices and we consider her one of us."[9]

A third theory was that DeAngelo had a mental health disorder called dissociative identity disorder (DID). This may have caused him to have two different identities. After his arrest, DeAngelo spoke about "Jerry," a voice in his head that he said made him do violent things he did not want to do.

An expert in criminal behavior dismissed the theory that DeAngelo had DID. Mental health professionals also emphasize that most people with DID are not violent. None of these theories about DeAngelo's motivation led to leniency in sentencing.

Another unanswered question was how DeAngelo managed to live in society without attracting suspicion. DeAngelo's neighbors in Citrus Heights gave various accounts of his behavior. One girl who was friends with his granddaughter said that DeAngelo had been nice to them.

Not everyone agreed. Other neighbors said DeAngelo was an angry man prone to outbursts, threats, and profanity. One family said DeAngelo called to threaten them because their dog barked frequently.

DeAngelo and his wife, Sharon Huddle, separated in 1991. Huddle did not file for divorce until after DeAngelo's arrest as the Golden State Killer. During DeAngelo's sentencing, Huddle submitted a victim impact statement to the court. In the statement, she wrote that she had trusted DeAngelo's excuses for his frequent absences.

One of DeAngelo's daughters submitted a five-page letter in his defense. She described DeAngelo as a loving, involved, compassionate, and hardworking parent. His niece also submitted a letter for the defense. She wrote, "I personally feel that someone else is inside him who I do not know."[10] One of DeAngelo's coworkers said that

HEALTH QUESTIONS

DeAngelo arrived to court proceedings in a wheelchair. Prosecutors, police, and victims believed DeAngelo did not need the wheelchair and that he was using it to appear frail and vulnerable. They believed it was another example of his ability to lie. A video of DeAngelo in his jail cell supported their claims. The video showed DeAngelo exercising and moving easily in his cell. DeAngelo's lawyers said the wheelchair was a tool in case court security officers had to move him quickly from one of the proceedings.

he didn't think the DeAngelo he knew could ever have committed those crimes.

After his known crimes ended, DeAngelo worked as a truck mechanic for a supermarket chain. He held the job for 27 years from 1990 to his retirement in 2017. He had friends at work with whom he ate lunch, fished, and water-skied. Many victims, their families, and prosecutors called DeAngelo a skilled liar who used his family and work as masks to avoid detection.

Cultural Impact

The Golden State Killer case has been the subject of many podcasts, books, and a documentary series. Interest in the case comes from the scope of the crimes and the unanswered questions about DeAngelo's motives and ability to hide his crimes. The new investigative methods used to identify DeAngelo with genealogy websites also drew in people to learn more about the case.

Companies had designed genealogy websites for consumers to learn about their ancestry. Some people questioned whether it was ethical to use genealogy websites for police work, and they believed it could be a violation of privacy. Others argued that the websites offered public access to data. Supporters compared

In 2021, DeAngelo was transferred to a protective unit in Corcoran State Prison to protect his safety behind bars.

investigators' use of the public-access websites to other undercover police work in public.

Prison officials had to take measures for DeAngelo's safety because of the public interest in the case and the nature of his crimes. Thien Ho, the Sacramento County district attorney who worked on the prosecution, gave an interview about DeAngelo in December 2023. Ho said, "He obviously is in a protected unit because of his status. Because you can imagine he is, [or] would be, a target in prison because of the crimes that he has committed."[11]

Ho also said that DeAngelo had a job in prison and was healthy. Ho declined to give additional details. In 2024, DeAngelo remained in prison in California at the age of 78, serving the sentences that will last the rest of his life.

ESSENTIAL FACTS

TIMELINE

Nov. 8, 1945: Joseph James DeAngelo is born in Bath, New York.

May 14, 1970: The *Auburn Journal* announces the engagement of Bonnie Colwell and Joseph James DeAngelo. The couple will break up in 1971.

May 18, 1973: DeAngelo is hired as a police officer in the Exeter Police Department.

Sept. 11, 1975: DeAngelo shoots and kills Claude Snelling.

June 18, 1976: DeAngelo commits the first known East Area Rapist attack.

Feb. 2, 1978: DeAngelo shoots and kills Brian and Katie Maggiore in the only known murders during the East Area Rapist attacks.

July 1979: Auburn police chief Nick Willick fires DeAngelo for attempting to steal dog repellant and a hammer from a local store.

Dec. 30, 1979: DeAngelo rapes Debra Manning and murders her and her boyfriend, Robert Offerman, in Santa Barbara County.

May 4, 1986: DeAngelo rapes and murders Janelle Cruz, his last known murder victim, in Orange County.

2001: Investigators use DNA profiles to confirm that the East Area Rapist is the same person as the Original Night Stalker.

Apr. 24, 2018: Police arrest DeAngelo at his home in Sacramento County after matching his DNA to that of samples collected from the EAR and ONS attacks.

IMPACT ON SOCIETY

Joseph James DeAngelo committed 13 murders, approximately 50 rapes, and more than 120 burglaries in the 1970s and 1980s. He committed these crimes in 11 counties throughout California. Law enforcement and media gave DeAngelo various nicknames before police discovered his identity.

DeAngelo was known as the Cordova Cat Burglar, the Visalia Ransacker, the East Area Rapist, and the Original Night Stalker. Once investigators conclusively connected these attacks, DeAngelo became known as the Golden State Killer. DeAngelo committed some of the crimes while he worked as a police officer and while he started a family with his wife, Sharon Marie Huddle.

DeAngelo eluded capture for more than four decades. In that time, he worked a steady job for 27 years, maintained a home, and lived with one daughter and granddaughter. DeAngelo's double life left unanswered questions about his motives and his ability to avoid detection. Investigators used new DNA technology and online genealogy services to identify DeAngelo. The methods they used sparked debate about privacy rights and police investigations.

QUOTE

"People were concerned, and they had a right to be. This guy was terrorizing the community. He did horrible things."

—Special Agent Marcus Knutson

GLOSSARY

alibi

A defense that an accused person was with another person or people in a different area at the time of a crime.

bludgeon

To beat with a heavy object, usually one with a flat surface.

canvass

To check neighborhoods near a crime for witnesses, evidence, and information.

composite sketch

A drawing of a suspect created by an artist using witness descriptions.

DNA

Deoxyribonucleic acid, the chemical that is the basis of genetics, through which various traits are passed from parent to child.

escalation

An increase in severity.

forensic

Characterized by the use of scientific techniques to investigate a crime.

genetic

Relating to or controlled by genes.

leniency

Treating someone with less severity than they may deserve.

perpetrator

Someone who commits a crime.

prowl

To move stealthily through an area to commit crimes.

ransack

To search through in a damaging way for items to steal.

stakeout

A police operation in which investigators watch a home or other location and the activities of a criminal suspect.

task force

A specialized law enforcement unit that focuses on a specific crime or series of crimes.

victim impact statement

Presented at a sentencing hearing, a victim's account of the ways a crime has harmed them.

ADDITIONAL RESOURCES

SELECTED BIBLIOGRAPHY

Holes, Paul. *Unmasked: My Life Solving America's Cold Cases*. Celadon, 2022.

Rae-Venter, Barbara. *I Know Who You Are*. Ballantine, 2023.

Rossmo, Kim D. "Behavioral Profiling in the Golden State Killer Investigation: A Comparative Analysis." *Homicide Studies*, 17 Oct. 2023, journals.sagepub.com. Accessed 1 June 2024.

FURTHER READINGS

Mooney, Carla. *The Zodiac Killer*. Abdo, 2020.

Newquist, H. P. *Scene of the Crime: Tracking Down Criminals with Forensic Science*. Viking, 2021.

Streissguth, Tom. *John Wayne Gacy: The Killer Clown*. Abdo, 2025.

ONLINE RESOURCES

Booklinks
NONFICTION NETWORK
FREE! ONLINE NONFICTION RESOURCES

To learn more about serial killers, please visit **abdobooklinks.com** or scan this QR code. These links are routinely monitored and updated to provide the most current information available.

MORE INFORMATION

For more information on this subject, contact or visit the following organizations:

CALIFORNIA STATE UNIVERSITY, SACRAMENTO, DIVISION OF CRIMINAL JUSTICE

6000 J St.
Sacramento, CA 95819
csus.edu/college/health-human-services/criminal-justice

The Division of Criminal Justice prepares university students for careers in law enforcement.

SACRAMENTO BEE

1601 Alhambra Blvd., Ste. 100
Sacramento, CA 95816
sacbee.com

The *Sacramento Bee* is a local newspaper in Sacramento County. It provided coverage of DeAngelo's crimes and arrest.

TULARE COUNTY HISTORICAL SOCIETY

PO Box 295
Visalia, CA 93279
tularecountyhistoricalsociety.org

The Tulare County Historical Society is a nonprofit organization dedicated to preserving the history of the county and its cities. The Visalia Ransacker crimes occurred in one of Tulare's cities in the 1970s.

SOURCE NOTES

CHAPTER 1. HOME ALONE

1. Michelle McNamara. *I'll Be Gone in the Dark*. Harper, 2019. 109.

2. McNamara, *I'll Be Gone in the Dark*, 108.

3. McNamara, *I'll Be Gone in the Dark*, 110.

4. Cleve R. Wootson Jr. "The Final Hours of the Golden State Killer's Final Victim." *Washington Post*, 27 Apr. 2018, washingtonpost.com. Accessed 2 June 2024.

5. Shelby Danielsen. "Jacksonville Mother of Last Known Murder Victim of the Golden State Killer Breaks Her Silence." *First Coast News*, 12 May 2018, firstcoastnews.com. Accessed 2 June 2024.

6. "Crime and Justice with Ashleigh Banfield: Decades of Search for a Serial Killer." *CNN Transcripts*, 27 Feb. 2018, transcripts.cnn.com. Accessed 3 June 2024.

7. Alex Bell. "Golden State Killer." *ABC10*, 11 Dec. 2023, abc10.com. Accessed 2 June 2024.

CHAPTER 2. AN UNSETTLED CHILDHOOD

1. Stephanie K. Baer. "The Suspected Golden State Killer Witnessed Two Men Rape His Sister. It May Have Fueled His Rampage." *Buzzfeed News*, 14 May 2018, buzzfeednews.com. Accessed 3 June 2024.

2. Paige St. John. "Man in the Window." *LA Times*, n.d., latimes.com. Accessed 3 June 2024.

3. Benjamin Oreskes and Richard Winton. "Golden State Killer Suspect May Be Linked to Earlier Cordova Cat Burglar Attacks." *LA Times*, 11 May 2018, latimes.com. Accessed 3 June 2024.

CHAPTER 3. A BROKEN ENGAGEMENT

1. Janice Williams. "The Golden State Killer's Ex-Fiance Bonnie Colwell Says She 'Refuses to Wear the Blame.'" *Newsweek*, 3 Aug. 2020, newsweek.com. Accessed 3 June 2024.

2. Williams, "Golden State Killer's Ex-Fiance."

3. Vicki Gonzalez. "Golden State Killer: Former Fiancée Confronts Joseph DeAngelo in Court." *KCRA*, 20 Aug. 2020, kcra.com. Accessed 3 June 2024.

4. Paige St. John. "Man in the Window." *LA Times*, n.d., latimes.com. Accessed 3 June 2024.

5. Joseph Serna, Richard Winton, and Sarah Parvini. "As a Young Cop, Golden State Killer Suspect Was Aloof, Ambitious, 'Always Serious.'" *LA Times*, 1 May 2018, latimes.com. Accessed 3 June 2024.

6. Paul Myers and Reggie Ellis. "Story of the Year: California Killer Was Exeter Cop." *Sun-Gazette*, 2 Jan. 2019, thesungazette.com. Accessed 3 June 2024.

7. Sarah Parvini, Joe Mozingo, Richard Winton, and Joseph Serna. "Golden State Killer Suspect Lived a Quiet Suburban Life, with Flashes of Rage and Anger." *LA Times*, n.d., latimes.com. Accessed 3 June 2024.

8. St. John, "Man in the Window."

9. Reggie Ellis and Paul Myers. "Former Exeter Officer Arrested as State's Most Notorious Criminal." *Sun-Gazette*, 2 May 2018, thesungazette.com. Accessed 3 June 2024.

CHAPTER 4. THE VISALIA RANSACKER

1. Reggie Ellis and Paul Myers. "Former Exeter Officer Arrested as State's Most Notorious Criminal." *Sun-Gazette*, 2 May 2018, thesungazette.com. Accessed 3 June 2024.

2. Sarah Parvini. "For Visalia Police, Golden State Killer Suspect Is 'The Ghost We've Been Chasing.'" *LA Times*, 7 May 2018, latimes.com. Accessed 3 June 2024.

3. "Evidence and Analysis." *Visalia Ransacker*, n.d., visaliaransacker.com. Accessed 3 June 2024.

4. Ellis and Myers, "Former Exeter Officer Arrested."

5. "The Murder of Claude Snelling." *Visalia Ransacker*, n.d., visaliaransacker.com. Accessed 3 June 2024.

6. "Physical Descriptions of the Visalia Ransacker." *Visalia Ransacker*, n.d., visaliaransacker.com. Accessed 3 June 2024.

7. "Attempted Homicide: The McGowen Shooting." *Visalia Ransacker*, n.d., visaliaransacker.com. Accessed 3 June 2024.

8. Paige St. John. "Man in the Window." *LA Times*, n.d., latimes.com. Accessed 3 June 2024.

9. "Attempted Homicide: The McGowen Shooting."

CHAPTER 5. THE EAST AREA RAPIST

1. Tom Cleary. "Joseph James DeAngelo: 5 Fast Facts You Need to Know." *Heavy*, 7 May 2024, heavy.com. Accessed 3 June 2024.

2. Veda Febericht. "Rapist's Skill Is Called Key." *Sacramento Union*, 3 Nov. 1977, C1, goldenstatekiller.com. Accessed 3 June 2024.

3. "Inside the East Area Rapist with Carol Daly." *YouTube*, uploaded by Sacramento Sheriff, 26 May 2018, youtube.com. Accessed 3 June 2024.

SOURCE NOTES CONTINUED

4. "These Are the Crimes DeAngelo Pleaded Guilty To in Golden State Killer Case." *Sacramento Bee*, 29 June 2020, sacbee.com. Accessed 3 June 2024.

5. Daniela Pardo. "Original Detective in Golden State Killer Case Talks Changes in Sacramento Since 1970s." *ABC 10*, 30 Apr. 2018, abc10.com. Accessed 3 June 2024.

6. "Crimes DeAngelo Pleaded Guilty To."

7. Paige St. John. "Man in the Window." *LA Times*, n.d., latimes.com. Accessed 3 June 2024.

8. "Cold Case Killer: Help Us Catch the East Area Rapist." *FBI*, 15 June 2016, fbi.gov. Accessed 3 June 2024.

CHAPTER 6. THE ORIGINAL NIGHT STALKER

1. "Affidavit in Support of Arrest Warrant for Suspected Golden State Killer." *Los Angeles Times*, n.d., 39, documentcloud.org. Accessed 3 June 2024.

2. "These Are the Crimes Deangelo Pleaded Guilty To in Golden State Killer Case." *Sacramento Bee*, 29 June 2020, sacbee.com. Accessed 3 June 2024.

CHAPTER 7. COLD CASES

1. Whitney Woodworth. "Salem Man Recalls Obsessive Search for the Golden State Killer." *Statesman Journal*, 27 Apr. 2018, statesmanjournal.com. Accessed 3 June 2024.

2. Tina Dirmann and Daryl Kelley. "DNA Tests Link Slayings in 3 Counties." *LA Times*, 3 Oct. 2000, latimes.com. Accessed 3 June 2024.

3. Steve Chawkins. "30-Year-Old Slayings of Goleta Couple Linked to Serial Killer." *LA Times*, 5 May 2011, latimes.com. Accessed 3 June 2024.

4. "Inside the East Area Rapist with Carol Daly." *YouTube*, uploaded by Sacramento Sheriff, 26 May 2018, youtube.com. Accessed 3 June 2024.

5. "Visalia Detective Came Face to Face with 'Visalia Ransacker' Serial Killer in 1975." *ABC 30*, 26 Apr. 2018, abc30.com. Accessed 3 June 2024.

6. "Cold Case Killer: Help Us Catch the East Area Rapist." *FBI*, 15 June 2016, fbi.gov. Accessed 3 June 2024.

CHAPTER 8. CATCHING THE KILLER

1. "The Origin of Indago." *Indago*, n.d., indago.ai. Accessed 3 June 2024.

2. Nsikan Akpan. "Genetic Genealogy Can Help Solve Cold Cases. It Can Also Accuse the Wrong Person." *PBS News Hour*, 7 Nov. 2019, pbs.org. Accessed 3 June 2024.

3. Barbara Rae-Venter. *I Know Who You Are*. Ballentine, 2023. 122.

4. Rae-Venter, *I Know Who You Are*, 115.

5. Rae-Venter, *I Know Who You Are*, 126.

6. Rae-Venter, *I Know Who You Are*, 128.

7. Paul Holes. *Unmasked: My Life Solving America's Cold Cases*. Celadon, 2022. 258.

CHAPTER 9. SENTENCED FOR LIFE

1. "Hearing Transcript for Accused Golden State Killer Joseph James DeAngelo Jr." *Rev*, 29 June 2020, rev.com. Accessed 3 June 2024.

2. "Golden State Killer Arrives in Prison to Start Life Sentence." *NBC Bay Area*, 3 Nov. 2020, nbcbayarea.com. Accessed 3 June 2024.

3. "Hearing Transcript."

4. Elisha Fieldstadt. "Golden State Killer Joseph DeAngelo Sentenced to Life without Possibility of Parole." *NBC News*, 21 Aug. 2020, nbcnews.com. Accessed 3 June 2024.

5. "Impact Statement: Berwert." *CBS News*, n.d., cbsnewsstatic.com. Accessed 3 June 2024.

6. Emily Shapiro. "'Golden State Killer' Survivor Confronts Rapist." *ABC News*, 19 Aug. 2020, abcnews.com. Accessed 3 June 2024.

7. Sam Stanton. "Golden State Killer DeAngelo Gets Surprise Visit in Court: His Former Fiancee, Bonnie." *Sacramento Bee*, 20 Aug. 2020, sacbee.com. Accessed 3 June 2024.

8. Fieldstadt, "Sentenced to Life."

9. Vicki Gonzalez. "Golden State Killer: Former Fiancée Confronts Joseph DeAngelo in Court." *KCRA*, 20 Aug. 2020, kcra.com. Accessed 3 June 2024.

10. Don Thompson. "Apology at Sentencing Deepens Mystery of Golden State Killer." *Associated Press*, 21 Aug. 2020, apnews.com. Accessed 3 June 2024.

11. Alex Bell. "Golden State Killer: Prosecutor Looks Back on the Many Masks of Joseph DeAngelo." *ABC10*, 11 Dec. 2023, abc10.com. Accessed 2 June 2024.

INDEX

ABOUT THE AUTHOR

REBECCA MORRIS

Rebecca Morris is the author of several nonfiction books for students. She has degrees in English, international relations, and comparative humanities.